Advance Praise for *Beyond the Mask*

"Brian Walsh had to endure something truly horrifying to learn lessons that helped him live an incredible life. He shares them in this book, which is a gift to anyone who reads this inspiring, powerful, and engaging story."

—Jon Gordon, bestselling author of
The Carpenter and *Training Camp*

"This book is filled with real life wisdom that can help you be more, do more, and serve more."

—Nido Qubein,
President of High Point University

"Sometimes the best life lessons are learned from people who have gone through unimaginable hardship. Brian Walsh pushed through his tragedy to become one of the best leadership teachers, and his reflections and advice are invaluable."

—Dana Perino, former White
House Press Secretary

"I've been telling Brian Walsh for years that he needed to write a book. He did not just write one, but wrote a great one. My friend learned to live a life with a new face. And he now teaches us to do the same...to put down our masks, face ourselves and ignite a fire in our hearts to live, lead and love in a more burning way."

—Tommy Spaulding, *New York Times*
bestselling author of *The Heart-Led Leader*
and *It's Not Just Who You Know*

beyond
the
mask

HOW MY TRAGEDY SPARKED AN INCREDIBLE LIFE: LESSONS I MIGHT NEVER HAVE LEARNED

brian p. walsh

Post Hill
PRESS

A POST HILL PRESS BOOK
ISBN: 978-1-64293-418-2
ISBN (eBook): 978-1-64293-419-9

Beyond the Mask:
How My Tragedy Sparked an Incredible Life: Lessons I Might Never Have Learned
© 2020 by Brian P. Walsh
All Rights Reserved

Cover art by David Ter-Avanesyan, ter33design.com

Post Hill Press
New York • Nashville
posthillpress.com

Published in the United States of America

We are more disturbed by a calamity which threatens us than by one which has befallen us.

—John Lancaster Spalding

CONTENTS

PREFACE

New Orleans, Convention Center, June 2005. Waiting in the wing of a stage that looks out on an enormous hall.

I should be nervous. It will be only the second time I've talked publicly about my private self—the first time was a disaster—and in a few minutes I'll walk out on stage to speak before nine thousand people. Before I even open my mouth, anyone who knows me knows what has made my story worth telling. Anyone who doesn't can make a damn good guess.

I give speeches several times a year. Business workshops, finance-related conferences, addressing divisions of companies that think I can motivate them to be more profitable (or less unprofitable). There could be three hundred people in the room, or thirty. Nine thousand? This will be a first.

I'm not nervous, though. A bit jacked, sure. And distracted. I should be going over my opening—I'll be reading from a teleprompter—but instead I'm thinking about a mystery:

How is it that I'm one of the happiest people I know? After what I went through, how is that possible? When no matter how hard I may want to hide what I went through, I can't?

Me, happiest? Seriously?

Something is wrong with this picture.

Yet it's true. I'm never down in the dumps or hopeless. In fact, I'm usually happy. Overflowing with gratitude and upbeat to the point (as my wife will tell you) of overdoing it, involved to the point (as my kids will tell you) of trying to solve everyone's problems, and able to stay calm (as my business partner will tell you) when everything's going to hell.

I'm not patting myself on the back. I'm no better than anyone. There are so many people who do things I never could.

But I'm pretty confident in my self-assessment, which no one would have predicted after that night so many years ago. A lot of those who saw the damage didn't think I'd survive until morning. No offense, but I have a huge advantage over many people because I went through something gruesome, a waking nightmare, and somehow it did not ruin me. Do I know how I was able to do that? Looking back, yeah, kind of. You know the saying, "You can let the moments define you or you can define the moments"? That moment, those ten or thirty or sixty seconds—you can't fault me for losing track of time, and given the chaos, none of my brothers in arms could say exactly how long I was there, conscious and then unconscious—that moment was not going to define me, I don't care how awful.

I'm not looking for credit for coming out of that. I *do* want to understand it enough that others understand it, because I think it could be helpful.

I don't feel nervous but maybe I *am* bracing myself for the convention center crowd. I never get lost in a crowd. I often wish I could but I can't. It's okay. Look: I don't love walking through malls or along busy boardwalks, but I can handle it. Time made it easier. You adjust. (It's easier for me than for my kids, and Brian Jr. often wants to pop someone in the nose.) Most people look. For those that do, the second glance is guaranteed. The ones caught unawares—turning a corner or stepping out of a car or snapping out of a daydream—sometimes look as if they've been knocked back, as if they've been hit by something physical. Kids, little kids, bother me less than grown-ups because for kids, it's curiosity. No judgment. They simply want to understand. At an Eagles game or shopping with Mary Ann at Super Fresh grocery, when a child is close enough and still young enough to point and boldly address his or her curiosity ("What *happened* to you?") before Mom or Dad realizes what's happening, I wish the parent didn't feel embarrassed and mutter an apology I never asked for, or try to whisk the kid away. I usually say, "That's okay, ma'am," or "No problem, sir. I'd like to answer the question." And

I do. It's real simple. "I was a firefighter and I got hurt in a fire." One hundred percent of the time, the little girl or little boy is satisfied with the answer and usually looks away, done, onto something else strange in the world. Grown-ups? They rarely move on so easily.

I moved on long ago. The road I've been on since that night is a remarkable one, filled with great joy and satisfactions as well as considerable pain and difficulty, including four dozen reconstructive facial surgeries (my count may be off by a couple). I don't know how many people thought I could get where I am, *as* I am. Mary Ann believed in me practically before she even saw what I looked like. Huge credit to a woman who agrees to a lunch date with a guy wearing a mask. I know that each of my three beautiful, incredible kids—Brian Jr., Matt, and Katie—believed in me from the beginning, though for accuracy's sake, by the time the first of them showed up I was well on my way to whatever this event here in New Orleans means. When Brian Jr. was born, I had already lived with the effects of the accident for seven years. Every person who knew me when the accident happened thought it was about the worst possible thing ever, yet it was also—cliché alert—the best.

Waiting in the wing, I think back to the first time I spoke in public in such a personal way, a few months after the fire. I was invited to address a group made up mostly of firefighters, on the virtues of perseverance. Supposedly, I was a living example. Problem was, when I took off my mask mid-speech to show the audience what I was talking about, seven people passed out.

Not walked out.

Passed out.

A group of firefighters.

I hope that doesn't happen today. I don't expect it to.

Once I survived the damage done to me by the fire, I was left with a huge advantage over almost everyone I saw. It would make many things, big and small, so much easier.

Lots of people can't deal with the hand they've been dealt, and it's often not even that terrible a hand. Sometimes it is, way worse than mine. I appreciate that. But I feel bad for some of those who've been dealt a pretty decent hand. I don't mean that in a smug way. I truly do feel bad for them. I see them living in an unhappy, helpless way, certain it's out of their power to make things better. As if it's a settled thing and they're literally unable to get from where they are to where they want to be.

I know that journey is possible because *I* got from there to here. I went from seeing how "it" was treated by almost everyone around me—family, friends, co-workers, bosses, potential bosses who refused to be my boss (because what was the point?), and lots and lots of strangers—to how it's treated now, with so many people saying, "I never think about you that way." For those in my life, the ones from before and after, it's really not even a thing anymore unless I make a joke about it. I joke about it all the time. Some pretty rude jokes, too.

Still, without my face looking like this, I honestly don't think I would be where I am today. I'm not saying that, without the fire, I would have had no reason to smile or feel proud, that I would have enjoyed no success. I don't buy that at all. I *do* believe that I'm a better professional because of the accident—my business partner and I started an investment and insurance firm more than twenty-five years ago, and are now privileged to serve well over a thousand clients—and I'm a better father, better husband, better son, brother, boss, mentor, colleague, friend…a better all-around person because of it. My experience from the fire and the aftermath helped forge who I would be, which is someone I probably never would have been. Look: I don't say go get caught in a fire. (Like I need to say that.) Or invite calamity or any sort of adversity. But what I took from everything that followed made me a happy man, fulfilled and purposeful. Travel that road and they eventually ask you to address giant halls filled with people a lot handsomer than you, though not necessarily facing life the way they could.

So I can't quite call what happened to me a tragedy. A calamity, for sure. And there's stuff I'll always have to live with. Often I'm afraid to go to sleep. The daily stares. The crystals sitting at the bottom of my lungs that may wake up some day.

In the end, I did not resign myself to what I had permanently lost. I focused on the good things still to come, within my reach and control. Was what I did extraordinary? No. Was I better equipped to handle it because I was so young when it happened? Maybe, maybe not. At seventeen you have so much more to lose. But maybe it's easier because you're less set in your ways. The dumbness and elasticity of youth can work in your favor.

However I pulled it off, dumb or smart, conscious or accidental, the lessons I took from the fire are both universal and particular. What I learned helped me to feel comfortable in my own skin, something that so many people, despite their amazingly smooth complexions, struggle with every day.

I get it: it's not exactly breaking news that adversity can put things in perspective. Big whoop. Still, I was lucky enough to get my wakeup call, and not everyone gets one. And I learned the lessons the way life happens—not neatly, sometimes surprisingly, sometimes almost invisibly. I had to connect dots. Eventually, I found that the same wisdom that applies to success in one area of life—like family or friendship—applies to success in another—like business—and vice versa, though you may not see it at first. At some point, I realized that when we talk about our lives, the word "potential" can be a synonym for "story." Everyone's got potential. Everyone's got a story. The question is whether your story ultimately gets told the right way and whether it's you who's telling it. Everyone's got a story. Mine just happens to begin right there on my face.

But this is not the story of a face. It's the story of a life.

If I hadn't learned the lessons I learned, I still would have survived—but is that the point? Just surviving?

Really?

I wait in the wing, tapping my foot. Any moment I'll hear the introduction and then my name, and I'll walk out onto the stage, probably one of the great moments of my life, yet I wouldn't be here if not for the worst, scariest, most pivotal moment of my life.

That night didn't start out that way. It was actually a beautiful fall evening, still warm enough that we had our car windows rolled down.

PART I:
FACING FACTS

CHAPTER 1:

Flashover Flashback

When we are no longer able to change a situation,
we are challenged to change ourselves.
—Viktor Frankl

I loved firefighting—not just the adrenaline rush of fighting fires but the camaraderie, the chance to help people, the opportunity to be proficient at something. I was sixteen when I joined Levittown Fire Company No. 2, the volunteer unit for my hometown in Bucks County, PA, a thirty-minute drive from downtown Philadelphia, twenty if I was behind the wheel. Our company did search and rescue and suppression: go in, check for people, put out the fire. We were nothing but fire engines, called just "engines," meaning vehicles equipped to pump water. As their name suggests, ladder trucks carry the big ladders. We didn't have a ladder over thirty-five feet. If we needed one for a larger building, we had to call it in.

When I joined, partly because some of my closest high school buddies did, we were not legally allowed to enter a burning building until we were eighteen. Junior firefighters did setup and support work, brought whatever the regular firefighters asked—get me this, get me that. After the fire was out, we did cleanup. That's it. We were not allowed to operate the pump or use extrication tools.

Anyone who has ever fought a fire or been in any dangerous, fast-developing situation knows that things don't always go according to plan.

By the time I was seventeen and a half, I had helped put out around three hundred fires. We averaged two to three calls a day, and if you were on call and your pager went off, even if you were in high school English class, you went. Once, another one of the junior firefighters set off a false alarm so he would get paged and could skip class. His prank was discovered. He was kicked off the force.

I loved getting beeped. I loved being part of the company. I was never much of a student, partly because of dyslexia that no one recognized. It gets tiresome having people tell you you're dumb to the point that you start believing it. I was always in remedial something.

You'll be going out to the trailer (where remedial classes were taught).

You'll go to tech school.

It may not be your dream, but there's something out there for you.

I had been a bit of a jokester in Catholic school, which went through eighth grade, and Sister Saint Angela, a terrible human being, and I had many talks in the hallway, though she was the only one talking. Probably some of my behavior was due to my learning issues—me wanting acclaim, at least from other kids. But Catholic school in the 1970s was not a setting where anyone in authority was going to pipe up and say, *Hold on, what's really going on with this boy? Why is he acting this way? Could it be that he's being made to feel dumb—and he isn't really?* If I clowned around or didn't do something the "right" way, Sister Saint Angela would grab me by my hair and drag me across the room.

It didn't help that my brothers and sisters preceded me at the school, Queen of the Universe. My middle name wasn't officially Why Can't You Be Like Your Brother? but it could have been. I was the caboose of the eight-kid Walsh train: four boys, four girls. Sixteen years separated me and Marie, the eldest. My mother delivered a stillborn child between me and Renee, the next youngest and four and a half years older than me, so I truly was the baby of the family.

I'm told I was a cute little boy, a bit mischievous but not obnoxious. As the youngest, I was often target practice or the rag doll for the other boys, especially Ed. We had tile floors in the bedroom and the upstairs hallway, so Ed and Kevin would get me to run the slippery floor while they flung pillows to try to knock my feet out from under me. Actually, I had a great time doing that. But Ed would also put me out on the garage roof and shut the window, then go downstairs and report to Mom, "Brian's out on the roof again." Mom would come upstairs and yell at me. I would tell her I was out there because I got put there, and Ed, looking wounded, would reply, "Why would we put him out on the roof?" It was usually Billy who came to my rescue.

In school, English and math were the enemy. I was a good writer, but reading was my problem. I inverted letters and numbers. When I was in fourth, fifth, and sixth grade, I had to leave the main school building, cross the parking lot, and enter the dreaded trailer with the other remedial students, none of whom were close friends. Not exactly a self-esteem boost. In tenth grade at Neshaminy High School, I was told that I would rotate two weeks of every month at Bucks County Vocational Technical School, a trade school, because I was one of the shitty students (not the technical term, but it was implied). There we could at least learn a trade, though learning a trade back then was not considered undignified the way it is by many people now. In my first year at Neshaminy, I took shop classes like Small Engine Repair and Basic Electricity, but at Tech there were entire "majors," like Heating and Ventilation, and Air Conditioning. I did really well in the classes. I could use my hands. The kids at Tech were scarier than those at Neshaminy—lots of bullying, drugs, having to fight your way out of the locker room. But after the first year there, it was fine. And it's where I met Kevin Glasson, who quickly became one of my best friends.

What I learned at Tech was useful. Later, when I trained for and took the test for the fire service, I excelled, both with the physical and mechanical evaluations and also the written questions. (Though because I'm terrified of heights, perhaps because of those times I got put out on the roof, I white-knuckled the part of the test where I had to climb a one-hundred-foot ladder.)

I was a reliable firefighter, and a lucky one: in almost eighteen months I hadn't suffered injury. Neither had anyone else in Company No. 2. Part of that, maybe a lot of it, I credit to our training. Our company was founded in 1952 by former New York City Fire Department guys who set the standard for training. No one messed around. Sure, there were times we'd hang out at the firehouse together, even play an occasional game of pool, but the chiefs didn't like us sitting around doing nothing. They had us cleaning all the time. I cleaned and polished lots of diamond plate, the embossed, patterned metal on the tailboard and trim of fire trucks. We cleaned the axes and other tools. If we went on a minor call a block away, when we got back to the station the chief still had us clean the truck. There was always a hallway that could use a coat of paint. There wasn't much downtime.

The good thing was, you really knew the truck and your equipment. On calls, I usually stood outside on the back with one or two guys, even three. The truck held ten, max. When we arrived at a location, the junior guys were responsible for hooking up the engine to the pump, dropping the hoses (lines) where needed, and anything else we were told.

Kevin and I were good firefighters, as were the two other juniors. We already knew as teenagers that we wanted to run into a burning building, not away from it. We would do what it took to be known as the kind of guy other firefighters wanted behind them. We wanted to show we had guts and wouldn't leave you. The senior guys respected us—we were strong and we didn't cause trouble. I even got the ultimate compliment: a nickname. The older guys called me Bones for being so skinny.

By the fall of 1981, after a year and a half on the job, my most intense moment as a firefighter was pulling a dead body from a burned car. It was winter. We had arrived at a vehicle engulfed in flames. After we put it out, Jack Quinn, the chief, said to me, "Check the car for a body, the poor bastard." It was stiff, charred, like a log, past recognition. Later, the investigators came up with a likely sequence of events: the driver was smoking, flicked his burning cigarette out the window, and closed the window—except the cigarette never flew out but sailed into the back seat, which caught fire. The driver pulled over to put it out, but as he climbed into the back he accidentally pushed against the button on the side of his seat which, like many cars at the time, folded the seatback forward rather violently, trapping him. He couldn't get out and he couldn't put the fire out. With the windows closed, he was soon overcome by smoke. If it hadn't been winter, he might have had more time, and lived.

I threw up while pulling out the body. I threw up afterward.

On Friday night, October 23, 1981, early in my senior year of high school, I drove into South Philadelphia with my friend Mike Murtha and his dad to visit Mike's grandmother. On the way back to Levittown, we stopped at Burger King, then they dropped me off at my home at 14 Quaint Road, a cookie-cutter house in a cookie-cutter neighborhood, and I went to bed.

My folks struggled financially, but I don't know that you could call us poor. Working-class, sure. Things were tight. My father was always concerned about money. Our home model was the popular Jubilee—a two-story, four-bedroom Colonial like so many others in the tract-housing development we lived in, a mostly Irish and Italian section of Levittown called Quincy Hollow. Growing up, the four boys shared an upstairs bedroom, Kevin and me in one double bed, Ed and Billy in the other. One wall was slanted, angling toward the roof. The older you got, the more often you banged your head. We had a nice-sized space in the middle but not enough room for desks for all of us, though we kept the room neat. Anyone who grew up in a Jubilee knows the room I'm talking about.

It was almost two in the morning when I woke to the beeping of my Plectron pager. We were second call on a fire in Bristol Township, meaning it wasn't our district but we were coming in to help.

I was dressed and out the door in under sixty seconds and hopped in my mom's Toyota Corolla. I had Tom Petty on the cassette player and the windows open. It was a comfortable night, or very early morning really, warm for late October. As soon as I turned onto Woodbourne Road, I saw the orange glow in the distance, five miles away. Not all calls you go on are "active" fires, where some suppressive action is required. This one, no doubt about it, was active, the flames evident.

On my way to the firehouse I saw Bob Hunter, our captain, exiting the 24-hour donut shop called—what else?—The Donut Shop, at Five Points intersection. I lowered Tom Petty. "Hey, Captain!" I yelled out my car window.

"I think it's a big job," he called back to me, walking to his car.

At the firehouse I dressed and took my position on the truck, holding on to the back, along with a couple others. Seating was first-come, first-serve, except for the driver. We were first engine out.

It wasn't a long run. We crossed the intersection and headed down Edgely Avenue to Route 13. As we neared the site, we could see a "header"—fire and smoke spewing from the top floor of one of the Edgely Run Apartments, a sprawling complex of nine three-story buildings, each with about thirty apartment units. Closer, we could see that half of what we would learn was called Building A was on fire, the other half wasn't. The Edgely Fire Company, also a volunteer unit—as were most in the area—was first in. It was their "local."

Just because you see flames doesn't make it a terrible fire to fight. In fact, it can be just the type you *want* to fight. Any time you see fire when you pull up, it means the gasses and heavy smoke are ventilated, either through the roof or windows. You usually don't take the beating you do when the location is closed up.

There were two ways to get into the building: a stairwell in front, another in back. The Edgely men had taken the front of the building, where fire was visible. We would take the back. All the residents, fortunately, had been safely evacuated. The plan that quickly developed was for the senior firefighters to get up to the third floor, then work their way down the hallways to keep the fire from spreading, if that was a threat. We assumed the firewall would prevent or at least inhibit spreading. In most cases, that's a good assumption.

The immediate assignment for the juniors was to take the 3½" hose, which was a couple hundred feet long, and tie it around the hydrant.

Then we used a collar called a "reducer" to connect that line to the 1¾" hose. It was my job to bring the head of the narrower line to the firefighter in the stairwell entrance.

I didn't have my breathing apparatus. It was back on the truck. I wasn't expecting to go into the building. I wasn't legally allowed to. I focused on the jobs my brothers-in-arms and I had in front of us.

Meanwhile, our deputy chief, Johnny Glasson, Kevin's older brother, headed upstairs to see what exactly was going on. Even with a firewall to keep the fire from spreading, there was sizing up to do. Surveying the third floor, Johnny was glad to see that things didn't look too bad. He even took off his breathing apparatus. It was a little hazy. He described it much later as the way a room gets after someone has smoked cigarettes, but no big deal. Johnny headed back down to see both companies making progress.

Standing outside the building, though, something didn't feel right to him.

Johnny was one of the wise men of Company 2. At age twenty-eight, he had more than a decade of firefighting under his belt. He had received commendations for bravery. Now, he grabbed a firefighter and told him to bring an Eckert, or "Eck," hook—an eight-foot pole with a hook on the end, used to pull down or pull out ceilings, ducts, or air-conditioning systems.

"Follow me," Johnny told the firefighter.

Meanwhile, I had handed the hose to Captain Hunter waiting in the doorway—when suddenly he was called elsewhere.

When you look back at certain life-changing moments, it's sometimes hard to put your finger on the turning point. Often there is none. Lots of little things happen, one after the other after the other, minor stuff you don't take note of at the time. As he parted, Captain Hunter instructed me to take the hose up the stairwell. In the next instant I was "on the nozzle"—holding the front of the hose—walking upstairs, slowly, with a couple guys behind to help advance the hose. Our aim: Get it to the firefighters already on the third floor.

When I arrived up there, Deputy Chief James Mulholland of the Edgely Fire Company paired me with one of his men and told us to check the nearest apartment unit for "extension of fire."

It doesn't matter anymore that I should never have been up there to begin with. Or that my breathing apparatus was back on the engine. At the time I didn't think about it. No one did.

On the second floor, I heard later, Johnny Glasson and the firefighter with the Eck hook walked to the end of the hall, the other side of which was the contained fire. Above them was the part of the third floor that was not on fire—or so it seemed. Johnny told the fireman to pull down a section of ceiling—and right away they saw something really, really bad: flames burning above. The fire wasn't yet raging. Johnny would later describe it as being like an ocean that was mostly calm, just a little wavy.

The danger was clear, though: There were roughly ten of us firefighters, from both companies, up on the third floor. Johnny had just discovered fire burning *beneath* us, and we didn't yet know we might be trapped. The firewall had not done its job. By the time Johnny and the other firefighter got to the stairwell, everything went black for a second.

Yes, black.

It's called a flashover. It's not common. In all his years fighting thousands of fires, before and after that one, Johnny would say later that he had been involved in only two other flashovers. There had been one a year before in a commercial building. Fortunately, nobody was hurt in that one.

In a flashover, there's a very brief period where there's not enough oxygen to support combustion. There's blackness as gasses and superheated air gather.

Then something blows in. It could be a draft from the stairwell or a broken window. Suddenly there's more than enough oxygen, combustion occurs, and the fire erupts.

In a more "normal" situation, there probably would have been enough time from the moment of discovery of the fire lurking beneath us to yell or get on the radio to everyone upstairs to *Get out! Back out! Now, NOW!!*—

But it happened so fast. The fire raced down the hallway, temperatures reaching eight hundred to one thousand degrees. Someone said later that the stairwells acted like chimneys. Johnny and the other fireman ran out and down as fast as they could, yelling for more help.

Hell had broken out up on the third floor.

We all had radios, and there were guys outside and downstairs trying to get hold of us up there. But the flashover happened with a speed that is hard to describe and hard to believe.

The firewall, it turned out, did not go all the way to the ceiling, thus failing to confine the fire to one portion of the building and instead allowing it to hop to the adjoining section. The wood-paneling used in construction meant the fire was in the walls, too.

It felt to me like a train coming through. All the walls were in flames—and suddenly the firefighter I had been paired with was gone. I looked for him, frantic, but without my mask I began choking. *Holy shit, where is this guy? You never leave your partner! You're taught to NEVER LEAVE YOUR PARTNER!*

I wasn't just choking. Now I was beginning to burn.

Who knew where the fucking guy was. I had to get out. Bad, bad shit.

Outside, the companies were setting ground ladders for us third-floor guys who couldn't make it to the stairs but who could hopefully get inside an apartment unit to a window.

Downstairs and outside, Johnny put on his breathing apparatus and raced back toward the building. Chief Quinn grabbed him. "Do not go in! You can't go in!"

"Our guys are trapped, Chief!" Johnny said. "I'm going in!"

Another cardinal mistake in firefighting—disobeying an order—but I would be very glad Johnny did. As he started up the stairwell, he saw that even the hoses were on fire.

Some firefighters from the third floor had found stairs. Some had found windows. Inside an apartment unit, I felt my way through smoke and flames to a doorway. Even with fire burning, it was dark, and the dense smoke was overwhelming. My flashlight didn't help much. I felt for where a window might be, but I was forced to the floor. The walls were engulfed by flames. I was blinded by smoke. Staying put was not an option. I needed to find the doorway that would lead me to the hose, to help guide my way out and down. As I moved, I touched my face—and realized I was touching nerve endings. I heard an agonizing scream. It took me a moment to realize it was me.

I was crawling when I found the doorway, got outside the apartment, and made it into the hallway. Now I had to get to the fire door for the stairwell. On my stomach, I leaned my shoulder into the big metal door to get it open, to safety, to clear air. As I opened it, the cold air in the stairwell rushed up and hit my face.

Another blood-curdling scream, only this one I don't remember letting out. Others heard it. Of course, I don't remember passing out.

Johnny, in the stairwell, heard someone yell from upstairs.

"I have someone here!" It was Kenny Sims, another one of our men, yelling. "There's someone trapped up here!"

* * *

I heard later how Johnny and Kenny, dodging flames, found me unconscious, the heavy hose on top of me. Kenny grabbed my upper body, Johnny my lower, and they got me downstairs and outside. The two of them knew they had brought someone out from Levittown FD, not Edgely, but didn't know it was me. There were no markings on my coat or helmet, no name to let them know who they had just pulled from the burning building. My head had swelled to the size of a pumpkin or a basketball, depending on who's telling the story. My face had suffered third-degree burns, the worst kind, over its entirety.

My good friend Kevin Glasson, who wasn't on call that night and had been at a birthday party for another of our crew, got word of "a bad apartment fire," and he and the others jumped in their cars and raced over to help. He was on the scene when they brought me out of the building.

No one was sure of the identity of the firefighter whose face was so horribly burned he was unrecognizable. At first they thought it was Skinny Keiluhn. They could tell the guy was thin. But a moment later,

Skinny came walking from around the corner of the building. Through process of elimination, they figured out it was me. Bones.

I was told much later that, off in the grass, some of my turnout gear—my gloves and my helmet, now melted to the shape of a dinner plate—sat there, smoking.

* * *

When exactly do we learn the lessons that become our guiding principles? If we gain insight from a trauma, were we always wired to learn that lesson, though maybe some other way, later on? And this terrible spark just got us to that wiser place *faster*? Can a person who doesn't ever go through that level of trauma really learn the lesson and benefit from its usefulness like the person who truly suffers, the person to whom it will stick forever?

* * *

Stop pouring water on my face! I thought.

Fred Schumann was the paramedic on duty that night, but I couldn't see him.

"Why are you doing that?!" I mumbled, or yelled, or maybe just thought. I was not exactly a reliable witness.

"Brian," he said, continuing to pour, "is that you?"

I recognized his voice. "Of *course* it's me, Fred! *What the hell are you talking about?*"

"We're taking you to the hospital."

The wailing of an ambulance had been incessant and steady. It dawned on me that maybe I was inside it.

"I don't need the hospital," I said.

"You're in shock, Brian."

"Let me get back out there."

"You're not going back out."

I faded out of consciousness.

* * *

The lighted ceiling was moving.

I was being wheeled into an emergency room. Chaos. I did not know why all these people were acting the way they were.

Someone on a phone call.

"We're not gonna do that!" he yelled. A doctor?

I could not make out the words on the other end, but they were being yelled, too.

"We don't want to do that!" the voice near me screamed back. "We'd rather get him to you!"

More garbled screaming on the other end.

The phone call was over.

The voice near me said, "We have to intubate."

His face—someone's face—loomed over me. *Am I on a gurney in a hospital hallway? Possible.*

"Brian, we have to put a tube down your throat to help you breathe," the face over me said, calmly. "You won't be able to talk after that." I had taken lots of smoke into my lungs, my esophagus. The heat.

Apparently I was given a sedative to make the intubation process easier. Strangers had entered my life. The person who had been yelling was a stranger. The person yelling back was a stranger.

* * *

Somehow, my parents were already there at Lower Bucks County Hospital, in Bristol Township. They came in and out of view, or I might have been drifting in and out. I was on oxygen. I learned that it wasn't water that Fred had been pouring on my face but saline.

My biggest concern, when conscious, was the back and forth of another phone call happening near my head, about a helicopter coming to take me somewhere.

I told you how I feel about heights.

I could not register a complaint, though, with a tube down my throat. I thrashed around, expressing my extreme displeasure with this plan. No one knew why I was jerking this way and that.

Suddenly the face of an unfamiliar older woman appeared over me. She looked stricken. I would later learn that her son, Tom Golden, age twenty-one, a fellow firefighter from Company 2, had suffered minor burns on his hands, plus smoke inhalation. Tom and I were the only two firefighters who had suffered injury at the scene. He was brought to the same hospital. When they call next of kin, they don't reveal the severity of the burns. So his mom had no idea what awaited her.

"Oh, my god!" the woman screamed, looking down at me with horror in her eyes. "Is that my son?"

"No," I heard my father answer, "but I sure as hell wish it was."

CHAPTER 2:

What the Hell Happened?

You were sick, but now you're well again,
and there's work to do.
—Kurt Vonnegut

At some point the night turned in my favor: fog rolled in. The helicopter couldn't get to the hospital to make the trip to wherever it was taking me. I had to be transported by a second ambulance.

What a relief.

But Fred the Paramedic was right: I was in shock. How naïve to think I had just dodged a bullet.

I was lucky to be alive. The external burns—not counting the potentially fatal smoke inhalation, scorched throat, and internal burning of my lungs from the superheated air—were horrendous, though I didn't know that yet. I learned that a doctor from the burn unit at St. Agnes Medical Center in South Philadelphia, where I now was, had been on the other end of the phone call screaming at a doctor at Lower Bucks, the one standing beside my gurney, convincing him that if he didn't immediately intubate me—run a tube through my mouth, down my throat to my lung, allowing me to breathe past my heavily swollen airway—I would not make it to Philly, never mind if by helicopter or ambulance. With facial burns like mine, the airways swell, obstructing breathing. I was not getting out of Bucks alive without intubation or tracheotomy. They finally listened to the burn center doctor and intubated and transported me.

When I arrived at St. Agnes, staff members awaited their newest burn victim: seventeen years old, full facial burns, mostly third-degree. Nearly 100 percent of my face and some of my neck were burned—nowhere else. I had had all my gear on except for my breathing apparatus. My head was now gigantic; fluid rushes to the part of the body that needs it. I was given lots of medication. Both of my eyelids were gone (left one completely, right one partly), but the swelling made that unknowable for now—and even if it was known, nothing could be done about it because my head was so swollen that my eyes were shut. As with almost every serious burn patient admitted, I was brought to the "tub room" and put in a huge tub where they scrubbed the burned parts. Apparently, I kicked up a storm from the pain. I don't remember. They dressed my face. Even with that careful process, infection remains a burn victim's lurking nemesis, often his killer. Your skin is your main line of defense against infection. Lose any of it and you become more vulnerable. Major infection can wreak havoc within hours.

I was moved to the intensive burn care unit, which was laid out like most ICUs. Closed quarters. Twelve stations. The unit had two sides—one for recovering patients, the ones in relatively better shape (though, face it, you're still in a burn ICU); the other for critical patients, those with the worst burns and in greatest jeopardy of infection, who might require ventilators. Two of the rooms on the critical side, 5 and 11, were "isolation rooms," with sliding glass doors that could seal them off completely.

I was put in Room 5.

When I was brought to St. Agnes, my parents were already there. They were both praying to God to see me through the night. The rest of the family was gathering, too. Heavily morphined, I drifted in and out, a terrible drifting. Whenever I woke, I fought sleep. I was deathly afraid that if I fell back to sleep, that would be it, my final moments of consciousness. My life would end. I was scared to death of death.

I remember holding hands with a parade of well-meaning family and friends. Everyone saying exactly the same sentence: *It's gonna be okay.* I couldn't talk, so I asked for paper and pen. I tried to write, *Stay here with me.* I tried to write, *Don't leave me.* When Kevin Glasson came in and held my hand, I gestured for the paper and pen. *What the hell happened?* I tried to write, and I guess I succeeded.

"It was a bad fire," he answered. "You got trapped. But you're gonna be alright."

After cleaning up the mess at Edgely, my firefighting brothers returned to the station and kept inquiring about me, then they began trickling in to St. Agnes. They had already heard that my chances of making it were small to none.

Small to none. As this book goes to press, it makes me smile to think that someday, when they're old enough, my granddaughters Ella and Joie are going to read those words.

* * *

St. Agnes was highly regarded. Doctors from all over the region spent time there to learn about treating burn patients. Some did a rotation there. A burn center ICU is like other ICUs in many respects except for the smell: the stench in a burn unit is frequently horrific. During my time there, some burn victims left on their own power, some died, some hovered in a life-death limbo. No one knew yet which category I would be in.

The burns I suffered were horribly painful. I don't know if I lost consciousness at the fire because the brain eventually does you the kindness of shutting down so that you're not "there" to experience that kind of agony anymore.

Yet that pain wasn't close to what I felt during wound-cleaning.

This excruciating ordeal was inflicted on me twice a day. The nurse would come in forty-five minutes before the process to inform me that I would be given as much morphine as the law allowed, enough to take the edge off but not to knock me out. They needed me awake during the nightmare. "We know this hurts," the nurse would say. At least they didn't try to bullshit me. When the nurse returned, she removed the bandages from my face, and scrubbed it all with a rough sponge-brush drowning in Betadine. One side of the weapon was sponge. The other, truly evil side, was brush, the side that really "debrided" the wound—removed dead skin that could be a source of infection. They cleaned the area thoroughly so that skin grafts, which they wouldn't attempt on me for ten to fourteen days, had a better chance to take.

They scrubbed every micro-inch of where I had been burned. Where it's deep, third-degree burns, there are no nerve endings anymore. Believe it or not, that's sort of a good thing: when they scrubbed there, it didn't hurt as much. On the edges, though, where the burns were second-degree or first-degree, there *are* nerve endings.

My god. Kill me now. I would not wish that pain on anyone.

It was a whole other definition of agony. It felt as if I'd been cut open and someone with a handful of wires was digging and scouring—which is pretty close to what they were actually doing. I could feel every fiber, every molecule, the tiniest exposed area teased and pulverized until I felt so raw that I prayed please, just please let me pass out from the pain, anything but this. Describing it now, decades later, the torture is still so vivid that there are tears in my eyes. When I've spoken with other burned individuals, they echo what I felt: those daily cleanings were more painful than getting burned, no question.

After the scrubbing, they washed my face with saline, then applied Silvadene ointment to help prevent infection, then wrapped my face again like a mummy.

They had to keep the environment germ-free, so anything from outside was strictly monitored. Visitors had to "scrub up" and "gown up"—wear gown, gloves, hat, and mask; only their eyes were exposed. Their belongings were kept in an outside room.

I don't think I yet comprehended how crazy with grief my family was, my parents were. My mother spent every minute she could at the burn center, though at first she was allowed to visit with me for only an hour at lunchtime and an hour in the evening.

She quit her job. *This* was her new job. It was still too soon to say if I would survive. She felt she couldn't leave the hospital, that if she walked away "something bad would happen." What had happened to me was bad, having me die was far, far worse. At one point during her vigil, she read a brochure about skin harvesting and donation. She walked purposefully to the desk and announced to the nurse, "I want to donate skin for my son."

The nurse gave her a kindly look, I'm sure. It could not have been the first time this misunderstanding happened.

"You do that only after you die, ma'am," said the nurse.

*   *   *

Of all the burn technician-nurses who cared for me, I really liked Connie L., who worked the day shift from 7 a.m. to 7 p.m., and Jim Noonan on the night shift. Connie had teenagers at home and was very motherly toward me. She knew how to calm me. Jim was friendly and funny, and great at wrapping faces; he taught the new RNs how to do it properly. He would also save my life three times.

I couldn't speak the first two weeks because I was intubated, so I had to write everything. But I also couldn't see: since most of the skin of my lids had been burned off, clips held the muscles of the upper and lower lids together. Sometimes, when I would write an instruction, Connie or Jim would say, "Sorry, *still* don't know what you want." Over time they got better at understanding, and I got better at writing more clearly. (Somewhere, I have a few of the notes I wrote.)

At times I was a good patient, other times I was stubborn. I didn't heed everything I was told. I'm not sure if it was because I was a teenager or because of my personality or my situation or some combination. I wasn't mad at any particular person at the hospital but just hearing I couldn't do this or that frustrated me. Like how they sometimes preferred I use the bedside urinal rather than the bathroom down the hall. Was it belligerence that I didn't want to pee in front of the nurse? I could get down the hallway. At first I needed help, but it wasn't exactly asking for the moon. Maybe I just wanted a base level of dignity. Maybe it was simply that I was in so much pain and surrounded by so much pain. And many of those around me were often screaming out theirs.

My parents and siblings were very supportive, with at least a couple of people visiting me daily. Each night, after my mother left the hospital following the second visiting hour, she called the nurse's station, wanting Jim to recount everything that had happened to me since she had left.

One night my mom was on the phone with Jim, checking in. From the nurse's station, Jim could catch just a glimpse of me, enough to see that I was kicking.

"Hold on, Marion, I have to deal with your pain in the neck son," Jim told her. It meant a lot to me and I'm sure to my parents, too, that he talked about me and to me like that, as if I was just another rebellious teenager. One of the first lessons I learned from my ordeal: *the small things get you through, especially when the big ones seem almost insurmountable.* "Brian wants something again," said Jim. "I'll be right back."

He turned my room light on to see that I had turned blue. I was struggling to breathe. A mucus plug had caught inside the endotracheal (ET) tube running from my mouth down to my lung, and the airway was blocked. Jim ran around the bed and started squirting saline into the tube and "bagging" me with an Ambu bag, pressuring the saline down to force the tube clear. He kept suctioning, bagging, suctioning, bagging, watching my face get bluer and bluer, until finally I coughed the mucus out of the tube. The blood rushed back to my face. I could breathe normally again.

Life saved, number one.

Two days later, Jim passed by my room to see blood shooting up out of my wrist, high enough almost to hit the ceiling and cascading down on me. My arterial line—an IV that leads directly into the artery and measures blood pressure and helps to tell how the lungs are functioning—was defective, and I was bleeding out. An adult has approximately seven minutes to bleed out before he or she is dead. Jim screamed for help while he sprinted to get a package of 4x4 gauze bandages for my wrist. The doctors sewed me up.

Life saved, number two.

I had nearly died twice within forty-eight hours. It was still anyone's guess the kind of burn patient I was going to be—one who walked out with some sort of a life still ahead of him, or one who didn't.

There were small accomplishments during recovery—getting from bed to chair by holding on to the rail apparatus, then graduating to making it all the way down the hall unsupported. By that point you'd think I would have appreciated how much my life had changed forever. Technically, I wasn't in shock anymore.

But come on. I was.

* * *

Even when things are going well in an ICU, you never get the sleep you need. There's the incessant beeping of monitors and ventilators, a drumbeat you're aware of even more in the middle of the night. Drugs wear off. Drugs are re-administered. Nurses poke you at all hours.

Then there's the screaming.

A patient named Milton was in Room 11, the other sealed-off room, which I could see a little bit from my room when I was out of bed. Because of the issue with my eyelids—no skin, but clips on the lid muscle tissue—I had to keep my head back to see anything. Swaddled in bandages, I needed just the right position to glimpse Milton.

Yet it was not the visual that stuck. It was his sound. He screamed. He screamed all the time, it seemed. You could hear it through the closed door. He was so badly burned—torso and legs, though not face—that he had to be suspended away from any surface. His mother would sit with him, and once when his door was open, I could hear her saying, "Milton, you're okay, you're okay," trying to convince him and her both. The nurses would give him more and more medication to do for him whatever they humanly could, and Milton would calm down and go quiet for a brief period. Then he would start up again.

I screamed occasionally—not all the time like Milton—but no one could hear me with a tube down my throat.

I heard Milton screaming and moaning hour after hour, day after day. Then one day I didn't hear him. Naïvely, I thought, *Finally getting some sleep, Milton. Good for you! And thank God.*

A moment later, a commotion. Keeping my head back to see out, I watched as a blur of doctors and nurses rushed toward Milton's room.

He was dead, of course. The only way he was ever going to be relieved of his pain was by the gift of death.

It took a beat or two before it dawned on me: *I may not be screaming out loud all the time, but that could have been me.*

Another patient, a young woman who had burns on 100 percent of her body—you read that right—was being cared for as best as possible by Jim. The woman and her two-year-old son had been in a car accident on the Schuylkill Expressway. The car had exploded in flames. She was in a special bed at St. Agnes, covered in plastic, and the burn technicians had to work through the plastic to get to her. At one point, her nose fell off. Her mother would sit on the floor of the hospital room, screaming that God should take her, though you couldn't tell whether by "her" she meant her daughter or herself. Probably both. Every parent in such situations experiences double the agony, at least.

What made the burned woman's situation so much worse—could it really be worse?—was that she was conscious during her dressings. My god, the pain she must have endured defies comprehension. The woman would mouth to Jim or the other nurse, "How is my son?" She didn't know that he had died at the scene.

She died, too. There was no way she could survive. There is a formula they use to predict, more or less, your chance of surviving a fire: take your age, add the percentage of burns over your body, and you get the approximate chance you'll die. (That's not exactly it, and other factors go into the calculation, such as gender, presence of inhalation injury or "full-thickness burn," which means third- or fourth-degree—but you get the idea.) So if you're 40 years old, and you have burns on 60 percent of your body, that's 40 plus 60…which equals 100. There's a 100 percent chance you're going to die from your burns.

If you have burns on 100 percent of your body, it doesn't matter how old you are. The woman had zero chance of living.

Technically, I was burned on "just" 4 percent of my body—though they were third-degree burns, and they were over the part of the body that everyone sees first, the part we look to when communicating, when expressing love and pain, the part everyone remembers, the part that does the most to convey who you are. Everyone's calling card.

True, 4 (percent) plus 17 (years old) may equal "just" 21, but mere survival is not what a 17-year-old is interested in. He wants to really live. To accomplish great things. He wants to fall in love, get a good job, start a family, maybe start his own business, make a name for himself. At seventeen, he hasn't begun to show what he can do. He wants to be remembered, and not for this.

* * *

I was intubated for fourteen days. After ten they tried to extubate me. As soon as they removed the tube, my throat started closing up, so they immediately re-inserted it. But two weeks is about the outside limit before the chance for infection skyrockets, and four days later they removed the tube in the morning, hoping I'd be able to breathe on my own. If my throat closed up again, they would immediately have to trach me by cutting a hole into my throat through the front, near the Adam's apple.

I must have been living right. The throat stayed open. I could now eat through my mouth. I could have conversations, and tell Jim and Connie exactly what I wanted, though the first couple of days my voice was hoarse. I was getting stronger. The swelling of my head had subsided considerably. I was still going through the hell of twice-daily cleanings and dressings of my facial wounds.

Through it all I had no idea what I looked like. One thing you can't find in a burn unit, not without effort, is a mirror. If your face has been severely burned, they don't come over to your bed after you've acclimated for a few days, undress your bandages, put a mirror to your face and say,

"Guess who? You, from now on!" My mask of white bandages covered everything but my mouth, the bottom of my nose and my eyes.

I was moved to a room on the other side of the ICU, the less critical half. The nurses encouraged me to walk more, though I still had someone accompanying me. Sometimes my goal was the restroom down the hall. It had a mirror. I was told not to remove the dressing because of the damage it could do, and I knew how painstaking it was to put on. Instead, I looked for long stretches at my reflection in that mirror. A mummy but alive. I was wrapped clean and tight. I was not going to mess with the nurse's expert job. Skin grafting would soon begin, and between how I was healing and the surgeries, I was sure my look would improve greatly.

Some of my firefighter brothers were more uncomfortable visiting than others. Could you blame them? Ending up in a burn unit is every firefighter's nightmare, the nightmare of everyone who loves a firefighter. When you're in that line of work, you know you're going to see death and carnage. You never want to see it happen to anyone. You never want to see it happen to a brother fireman. I could tell how tough it was for Johnny to be there—not just because of what happened to one of his comrades but also because he was one of five Glasson boys who were firefighters. He left a St. Florian medal on my bed. His mother had given it to him. St. Florian is the patron saint of firefighters.

The guys told me the investigators for the Edgely fire determined that there were two things, really, that caused the fire to spread the way it did: firewalls that didn't go high enough, plus the use of flammable wood paneling in the building's construction. The owners were cited for these and other code violations literally days before the fire. The source of the fire was unclear. Was it careless smoking? Careless cooking? All they knew was that it had broken out on the third floor, destroyed the entire building, and caused hundreds of thousands of dollars in damage. It didn't appear to be arson, though there was an incident the very next night, same complex, Building F, which *was* arson. About forty residents had been displaced by the fire we fought, and the Red Cross and the building owners were working to find them temporary housing.

Would I be in a different situation if I had had my breathing apparatus on me? Almost definitely—but we were still dealing with a flashover, a very rare occurrence. It was easy for me to slip into "what if" thinking, especially lying in a hospital bed or sitting in a chair most of the day, day after day, with no school or work obligations, with a single window to look out on the world. What if the building owners had built proper firewalls? What if they had not used wood paneling? What if the code violations had been caught months earlier, and the owners had fixed them? What if the two volunteer fire companies had been more careful about sending in a junior volunteer? What if junior volunteers had coats or equipment more clearly indicating that we were off-limits? What if I had refused to take the hose up the stairwell to the third floor? What if I hadn't been on call that night?

What if. What's the point?

I wasn't the only one under eighteen on the scene. I was an able body, a needed body. Wrong place, wrong time. No one had done anything maliciously. It didn't help to Monday-morning-quarterback it. Or to resent that it happened at a fire not even in our district. You commit to helping, not to keeping score.

Some of the local newspapers couldn't do even that. Days after the fire, the cover headline in the Bucks County paper read "TOWNSHIP MANAGER SAYS FIREMAN'S INJURY NOT COVERED UNDER WORKMAN'S COMP BECAUSE HE WAS UNDER 18." My father read that one right after coming home from a visit at the burn center. Outside of my name and age, the paper got so many details wrong ("minor burns" especially stands out). But the gist was right: the township's insurance company was going to fight covering the cost of my injuries because I was underage.

At the burn center one morning, a social worker sat down in my room to ask me a bunch of questions. Some of them seemed dumb, some intrusive, some pointless.

The next time Johnny visited, I handed him his St. Florian medal. He refused. "You never know when you'll need it," he said.

Free of the ET tube and able to eat on my own, I didn't want to. The food was inedible. I went on a non-religious, non-political hunger strike.

Occasionally I would drink Ensure, a high-calorie beverage, sometimes in an orange-flavored version, but it wasn't enough. And because of the high risk of infection in a burn unit, outside food was disallowed.

Jim Noonan kept telling me I had better start eating. Calories were crucial to help heal the burn, the skin, the body. I needed something to fight with, and without food I was making it much harder on myself. "As a teenager you're not used to eating this kind of food, I get it," he told me. I couldn't tell if he was prodding me or commiserating.

After yet another day of not eating hospital food, I started to show weight loss. Bones living up to his nickname. That night, Jim came to my room, closed the door, pulled the curtain closed dramatically, and in a voice just above a whisper, said, "Brian, they're worried about you. What can I do to get you to eat? Tell me. Because if you don't eat, you *will* die."

I was intrigued by his whispering and the closed curtains, like we were plotting something. Like he was saying to me, *Everything's on the table—crazy ideas, illegal ones, whatever. We've just gotta fatten you up.*

"When they get to your bed during rounds," he continued, "the doctors and nurses see you're not getting your caloric intake. The tube is out, you're able to talk, you're able to walk, you're able to use the restroom down the hall, but if you don't eat—"

"I want McDonald's," I said, but quietly, so only Jim could hear. The nurse's station was not far. "I want a Big Mac and french fries and a milkshake."

Jim nodded. He knew, as did I, that if he got caught bringing in something from outside, given the tight controls, he would probably be fired.

The next night he smuggled in McDonald's. "Please don't let the nurses see this," he pleaded, as he removed from his backpack a white bag with the familiar yellow M and red highlights, "because they'll rat on me." Jim brought me McDonald's the next night, and the next. I devoured it all, while continuing to reject the hospital meals. A few mornings later, with Jim at the end of his night shift, the doctors came by on their rounds as I slept. They noticed I was gaining weight.

"How is he doing that when he isn't eating?" one of the doctors asked, looking to his equally puzzled colleagues for an answer. The doctor looked at Jim, who shrugged.

He kept bringing me McDonald's. My life was more important than protocol, he said. He pointed out that this was the third time he had saved my life.

He told me that so long as I was Irish, stubborn, and absolutely determined not to eat hospital food, he would be forced to keep bringing me Big Macs.

* * *

Let's talk a moment about my face, in particular, and burned skin, in general.

As Jim said to me later, without much sugarcoating, "If you put bread in a toaster, and burned it to the point where you couldn't burn it anymore, that was your face. Scary to everyone else but not to those of us in the unit."

He told me he had seen professional football players come to visit family in the burn unit, and before long these big strong guys, people who knew violence up close, who knew what tearing and snapping and ugly bending does to human body parts, were passed out on the hospital floor.

Despite my daily walks down the hall to the bathroom, I hadn't once looked underneath the bandages. I hadn't asked to peek in a mirror when they were re-dressing my mask. I was too busy willing myself past the incredible pain of the wound-cleaning. I believed I was going to look like I did before the accident. Close to it, anyway. How did I convince myself of that? Maybe I was no genius, but could I seriously not understand what was in store for me? Really?

The most exciting thing about the start of the grafting process was that it meant less skin area exposed, meaning the twice-a-day cleaning/disinfecting process would cover a smaller area, causing a shorter amount of unreal pain.

The graft would be for my full face, to be done in two phases. They would harvest skin from my thigh, a strip from knee to groin. They would fasten what looked like a roach clip at either end of the thin piece of skin they removed, cut out the strip, remove the skin with the clips and submerge it in alcohol. They would then place the strips on my face, one by one, like bacon in a skillet.

For the operation I would need to be intubated again. They gave me a paralyzing agent so my leg wouldn't move during the harvesting, and anesthesia to put me to sleep.

That was the plan, anyway.

At some point during surgery, I woke up. They were cutting skin from my right thigh. I could feel the pressure of the slicing. I screamed, or thought I did—or maybe I tried and no one could hear me because I was intubated. And it didn't help that with my eyelid skin burned away (the muscle tissue remained), my eyes remained basically open when I was sleeping. But here I was, mid-operation, very much awake. *You have got to be kidding me,* I thought as I lay there. I knew there was a delicate art to managing anesthesia over a long surgery. Mine was supposed to last about eight hours. I also knew I was in the midst of a waking nightmare.

I guess I lost consciousness again soon after.

In the recovery room, I gestured for paper and pen and wrote:

I woke up during the surgery

The doctor read the note.

"Nope," he said, dismissing my statement and me by directing his answer to my parents. "Didn't happen. People often have dreams during surgery about waking up. He didn't actually wake up."

It was a lie. And he knew it. Because there was a commotion in the OR when I woke. My blood pressure shot up. I remembered.

Later, the social worker assigned to me, John, came to my room. "Hey, I hear you said something about waking up in the OR. Can you describe it to me?"

I did. He looked at my mother, nodded, and said, "Yep, he woke up. No one would know that level of detail."

Why was it even a question?

I didn't blame the doctor or anesthesiologist. I understood that dealing with trauma is messy, almost always messier than we acknowledge or talk about. Nothing goes smoothly, ever. If it did, I wouldn't have been in the burn center in the first place. A fire that looked manageable when we pulled up in our engine turned out not to be. These medical people were all doing what they could to save my life. But I knew what I knew. I didn't appreciate the doctor covering his ass and denying the truth. Plus, he should have been open enough to admit it so maybe they could tweak things and reduce the chance it might happen to the next poor soul.

We didn't know if the graft would take. Many don't. The skin falls off. The doctor said we would wait a week or two for the next one.

Because of the amount of skin removed from my leg for my face, my leg was now hard to straighten. Charlie, my "burn aide," would constantly yank my leg straight, a wrenchingly painful move. He encouraged me to put my leg down and walk on it. He yelled at me. I yelled at him.

During all this I was lucky to have Connie and Jim. I felt I could tell them anything. Connie treated me like a son. Jim talked to me about what it might be like when I returned to school. He got me to open up a little bit about what he called my "fears," about being a seventeen-year-old kid who had been in a bad fire and now had to face the world. I didn't know what I looked like, still, but I was confident I would look much, much better after the grafts and the healing. Even so, I once referred to myself as a monster.

"You're not a monster," Jim said. "You're burned."

When I told him details about the fire, he said I never should have been sent in. That I was only a junior volunteer fireman. From what he had heard, it was probably a giant ball of fire in the adjoining space that had knocked me over into unconsciousness.

Jim told me about his kids, who were around my age. He told me that face and hands are among the most serious burns. With the former, it's usually accompanied by pulmonary burns; with the latter, it's difficult to restore full function. He told me he was a maestro especially at wrapping hands. He hadn't had to wrap mine, which weren't burned.

I told him that the night I got burned was the first time my father ever said he loved me, in the ER at Bucks County Hospital. I didn't recount it to Jim with shame or bitterness. I knew my dad wasn't an "I love you" kind of person. I must have been impressed by the undeniable magnitude of the moment, that it actually got him to say it.

Sometimes I shared with Jim my sadness over what had happened. I acknowledged I had "worries," maybe an easier concept for me to swallow than "fears." But didn't every teenager?

One morning, without my knowing, John (the social worker) cornered Jim. "Do you think Brian's suicidal?" asked John.

"No, I don't," Jim replied. "What makes you say that?"

"Well, a seventeen-year-old whose life is upended like this? He was probably dating before this happened. And enjoying his friends. And playing sports. Now look at him. He'll be wearing a mask for years."

"But he's strong," said Jim. "Brian never mentioned anything to me about being depressed. He never sounds depressed. He wants to get out of the burn unit. He wants to get on with his life."

I didn't know about that conversation until weeks later, after I was out. Nor did I know that social worker John, though meaning well, had gone to my high school to talk to the administration and my teachers and even my classmates. He told them that when I eventually returned, they shouldn't stare or point. Did they really have to be told that? He told them that they should try not to make me feel out of place. He thought he had to prepare them for me, as much I had to be prepared for the world. I was mixed about whether to feel angry or grateful for his efforts.

Maybe it was standard to do that. Maybe I forced it because I had been so unenthusiastic about the repeated offers to talk with someone about how I felt about my experience—therapists, social workers, nuns. Can you blame me? One therapist walked in and said a few things he thought would encourage me, but I can't remember a single one of them because he also said, as if it was fact, that I would probably never work anywhere with people.

And my religious faith certainly wasn't helped by a staff nun who asked me to thank God for the pain and suffering I was going through. I kid you not. I couldn't tell her what I thought of the suggestion because I had a tube down my throat when she said it. When I finally could speak, I said some pretty nasty things to her, which I regret. (No, actually, I don't.)

Eighty percent of the first graft "took." Ten days later they performed a second graft, addressing the areas that didn't take. It was not my final graft, not even close, but the last one they would perform at St. Agnes before discharging me.

I had been in the burn unit almost a month and my time there was coming to a close, it appeared. Still, it was a burn unit. There was always time for something to go wrong.

One day, I walked with a nurse down to the restroom at the end of the hall. I used the toilet. I washed my hands. I looked in the mirror. The mummy stared back.

This time, the mummy did not turn away. He needed to see what he looked like underneath.

Slowly, against all wishes and protocol, I began to undress my bandages. Carefully, extra slowly, strip by strip, I peeled it off, until finally I could see—

The door opened, fast. I had been in there too long and the nurse must have figured out why. She yanked me away from the mirror and out of the bathroom.

I did what I think anyone would after looking at him or herself, if that was what they actually looked like.

I cried.

* * *

Don't google "facial burns" unless you've got a strong stomach.

People who have never gone through it are eager to tell you "it will get better," as if they know. They mean well. Maybe they even have a relevant experience to share with you—about a doctor or nurse or therapist or hospital or rehab or scarring or searing pain. But none of the people in my life who encouraged me and offered advice had ever been burned, certainly never across their whole face. Who were they to tell me what this felt like right now and how different it would feel in the future? Having them say "it will get better" was like a man telling a pregnant woman that the pain of childbirth isn't so bad. When others were cheer-leading, I often just wanted to tell them to fuck off. But there was no one in particular who deserved such a reaction. It was more something I just wanted to release.

* * *

The threat of infection in a burn unit is constant. I think I've made that clear by now. Infection is often the thing that takes you out, though there are cases like Milton and the woman in the Schuylkill car accident where the burns are flat-out unsurvivable.

The end of my fourth week at St. Agnes, an infection spread through-out the burn unit. At first the hospital did not know how it was travel-ing. Every patient was affected, including me.

My fever got so high I became delirious. I hallucinated I was falling off a tall building, over and over. My mother and my sister Renee sat with me as much as they could. For four days I was completely out of my mind.

The only area in the hospital affected was us, the burn unit. Yes, it makes sense that infection, some infection anyway, can pass from person to nearby person. But it was curious the way the outbreak was severe, yet also contained. And the staff was so careful about keeping individual patients free of outside contaminants. Finally, the hospital authorities realized that the source had come through the burn unit's HVAC system, which was separate from the rest of the hospital's. Bacteria called pseudo-monas was probably the culprit. It had traveled through the ventilation system, like some horror film, right into the burn unit, which was so meticulously shielded from external contamination. Healthy people can handle exposure to low levels of pseudomonas. Burn patients can't.

They had to move us away from the exposure. They scrambled for beds for us and found one for me in the pediatric wing. I felt strange there, an almost-grown man among all these little kids.

My fever had broken, and I was no longer hallucinating. I was truly the lucky one.

I don't mean *one* of the lucky ones. The lucky *one*.

There had been twelve patients in the burn unit, including me. A little more than one week later, there was just me. Over the course of a week, eleven of the twelve burn patients died from infection. I was the lone survivor.

Had my youth helped me? Or the fact that I was on my way to "recovery" when the outbreak happened? I don't know that I believe in this sort of thing, but at one point I did think of the St. Florian medal that Johnny Glasson had insisted on leaving with me because "you never know."

The burn unit would open back up a month later, after I was discharged from the hospital.

I had been at St. Agnes for just over five weeks. I thanked Jim and Connie for everything they had done. They had helped to show the good in people. There was so much that I lost, so much I unintentionally exposed myself to and jeopardized by not having my breathing apparatus and mask, so much that changed for me the moment I went up that stairway with the 1¾" hose to help my fellow firefighters deal with a chaotic situation.

When I left St. Agnes, I wondered: Should I consider myself lucky? Unlucky? Blessed? Cursed? Like it or not, my life would be thought of, by everyone else and probably by me, too, as Before the Fire and After the Fire. How could I possibly make After the better of the two halves? Though they weren't really halves. The After part would probably last a lot longer.

So…now what?

As I faced an uncertain future, who would I be in it? Did it make sense to create a whole new persona? I can't say that on October 23, 1981, the day before my accident, I had a real clear idea of what I wanted from life. How many seventeen-year-olds do? But it certainly didn't include the "challenges" I would now be facing.

What would it now include—marriage, children, professional success? Fast cars, world travel, girls? Probably not. But maybe. Where would I live? Would I have many friends or live a quiet life or be an absolute hermit? Would I have a job where people wouldn't have to see me or maybe even interact with me, as the jackass therapist had informed me? I can't say I had to re-adjust my plans since I didn't have them. But surely they would be different now.

Aside from the support of family and friends, I really had only one thing to go on: determination. I had always been a hard worker. By the time I was twelve, I had three paper routes around Levittown—the *Philadelphia Inquirer* in the morning, the *Bucks County Courier* and the *Philadelphia Bulletin* in the afternoon. Sometimes I walked the route, sometimes biked. And post-accident me wasn't changed in that regard: the small but important accomplishments I had made every day with the physical therapists and the occupational therapists showed what I could do if I put my mind to it.

Though I didn't yet know it, the benefit I got from that October night, above all else, was an education like no other. Because of that single episode, I was forced to confront things in other people, in the world, and most of all in myself—and to do so day after day after day, because I could not run away from the exterior scars that remained. Everyone could see them, all the time. That walk up the stairwell in the back of Building A, and everything that followed, shaped my personality and, more importantly, my character. Some days I can't bring myself to say I'm glad it happened—hey, how cool would it be for me to walk through a mall just once, unnoticed and unremarked upon?—but that's another key part of that education: learning how to not look back for more than a moment and think about what could have been. *What if...*nah.

I didn't think I would live through the night of October 24, 1981. No one thought I would do as well as I did. They gave me up for dead—figuratively, anyway.

Today, I've got many people who rely on me; quite a few consider me one of their go-to people, in good times and bad. If that's the arc of my life story, from there to here, it's a pretty damn good one, don't you think?

* * *

I wrote this book to share what I have learned through the lens of my accident, and how lessons that were so beneficial to me might be helpful to others. It's true that you can learn what I learned in other ways; nearly burning your face off and almost dying multiple times are not pre-reqs. But because my situation was extreme, I probably learned these lessons faster and deeper than I would have. Had I not gone through what I did, I might not have learned them at all. Sharing this acquired, fortunate wisdom is my main goal.

In Part I, I felt it was necessary to recount, to the best of my ability, what happened that night and in the weeks in the burn unit that followed.

Although the repercussions from the accident were not over when I walked out of St. Agnes—far from it—I feel as if I no longer need to give the blow-by-blow, at least not chronologically. In Part II, each chapter covers a different lesson or mindset about making the best possible reality. Some of the lessons that were important in guiding me are ***bolded and italicized***, a variation on some of the tools I learned to use when I was first diagnosed with dyslexia: Slow down. Be deliberate. It's really as much for me as for you.

From what I see, many people out there seem blessed with options, including ones that most of us would agree are really desirable. Yet so many people find it tough to get where they want.

For me, facing forward was really my only good option. And it worked.

PART II:
FACING FORWARD

CHAPTER 3 :

Unmask

The eyes can choose where to look.
—Ursula K. Le Guin

At seventeen, you're immortal. *Nothing's gonna happen to me!* You're not sure where you're headed or where you'll end up. When you get there, though, you're likely to think, *Wait, I never thought it would end up like **this***.

A firefighter looks reality in the face. But to do the job well—for anyone in a dangerous profession to do their job well—it's sometimes best *not* to look reality in the face. To not consider what might happen on the very next call. If you did, you couldn't do your job. So instead of confronting the worst possibility, sometimes it's better to rely on faith and denial.

That's how a lot of us live our lives. On faith, in denial. I'm not criticizing. Life can be brutal. Life *is* brutal. Other people can be so disappointing. As "strategies" for approaching life, faith and denial actually hold up pretty well—until they don't. Until one day you look in the mirror and the reality stares back—that face, which you see with your own eyes, is impossible to deny.

The upside of that, for me, was that I probably got a more accurate idea of what people thought of me than most people do for themselves.

I once saw an interview where Terry Saban, wife of the legendary college football coach Nick Saban, said something like, "Nick's biggest problem is he doesn't know how other people view him."

Seriously? Given Coach Saban's reputation as controlling and a perfectionist, that seemed like a pretty damning thing for her to say about her husband. I wondered if the comment was scripted, some kind of goof. The more I thought about it, though, the more fascinating I found it. Could it be that one of the most detail-oriented, hyper-aware successes really *didn't* know how he came off in public?

Of course it could! Because it's true of *most* people, successful or not. Because most people can't tell for sure what others think of them.

Not me. I've had my problems the last thirty-plus years. That ain't one of them.

* * *

Before I go further, I need to tell you about my mask.

A couple of weeks after I left the burn unit, I lay down on a cushioned platform in the office of my occupational therapist, Ruth, who gave me a straw to breathe through before she slathered plaster on my face, everywhere but the eyes, nostrils, and mouth. Within a couple of hours the plaster hardened into a shell, Ruth peeled it off my face, then sent the mold to a manufacturer, and within a week we got back a hard plastic mask, like a hockey goalie's. I wore it, with a pressure garment made of stretchy but tight fabric over it to apply added pressure, to keep the scars from keloiding—thickening and hardening, like rope left too long in the sun. I would need to wear the mask as long as the scar tissue kept growing. Every two months, Ruth and I went through this process, making a new mold, so that the mask could apply maximum pressure to the parts of the face that needed it most.

I also had a mouth extender, a metal bar with plastic at each end that could be cranked to widen, if needed. I inserted the contraption into my mouth, then expanded it until my mouth was sufficiently stretched, for the purpose of working the skin and muscles in and around my mouth so that I could talk and eat normally. Here, too, I would return to the doctor every couple of months, so he could evaluate how well my skin was stretching, and we would usually expand the device a little more.

I wore the mask approximately twenty-three hours a day, taking it off only when I ate, showered, or lubricated my face. I wore the mouthpiece when I slept, like a retainer. I wore both for two years.

If you think walking around in public with a disfigured face is tough, you should see the reaction to someone dressed as Jason from *Friday the 13th* when it's not Halloween.

* * *

I'm a pretty good judge of character. Is it because I literally wore a mask for so long that I felt like a walking camera, catching people letting their guard down when I was nearby because I didn't appear to be a full, normal person? Is it that, with or without a mask, I could see in people's eyes what they were thinking about me, and they couldn't hide it? Is it a salesman's trick, the ability to size people up in a few seconds? Is it being part of a big, complex family? Maybe all of it, maybe none.

How do people see you? Because ***if you can see accurately how people see you, then you should also be able to see yourself more accurately, or at least the part that others tend to focus on.*** How can you find that sweet spot, that valuable place where you see yourself neither as worse nor better than you are? Wearing a mask for two years gave me an advantage in all this. I might even call it, yes, a gift. People noticed me; they couldn't not. People stared. People wondered what horror lay beneath. Once, waiting at the Philadelphia train station with my mother, a woman in her early twenties came up to me, stuck her face right up to mine, and studied me, like I was something in a museum or a zoo. "What are you doing?" my mother snapped at the woman, who didn't have the decency to acknowledge that there was an actual human being behind the mask.

Some people looked at me with almost transcendent compassion.

The mask was extremely tight and could get physically uncomfortable. Add to that the shark liver oil rubbed on my face twice a day to keep the skin supple (though it was still so much more brittle than "real" skin feels like), and it took a while to get used to. The mask was also my companion and protector, my daily reminder, my truthteller. Yes, it was also hiding a truth. But the fact that I had it on, out in the world, said something truthful, too.

Wear an actual mask long enough and you get to thinking about the masks worn by others. Masks that are invisible, but not really. Masks that try to obscure a truth, but often reveal it at the same time.

I came to see that almost everyone wears a mask. For some it's a mask of overconfidence, to hide their insecurity. For some it's a mask of focus, to hide their fear of inertia or irrelevance or a general lack of purpose. For some it's a mask split in two, allowing them to say one thing to some people and a completely contradictory thing to others: people who "talk out of both sides of their mouth."

When I stopped wearing my literal mask, it wasn't easy. It was impossible to lie about my face. But whatever it looked like and whatever it said about me, mistakenly or not, I fought through it. I was done with masks. I wanted to be who I was, whoever and whatever that might be.

I imagine it's equally hard, maybe even harder, to stop wearing a mask you've been wearing a long time that's not physical. Maybe you didn't even realize you were wearing one, or that you wear it in certain situations. But it can settle and harden.

I try my best not to bullshit anyone. I know from my family and closest friends that I've succeeded at that maybe too much because, frankly, I'm not to everyone's taste. I can be hard for some people to take. That's a downside of being an extreme non-bullshitter. (Jim Noonan was right: I *can* be a pain in the neck.) The upside is living what feels like a more honest life, one where you're a lot closer to who you are, what you want, and who you want to spend time with.

Sometimes I marvel at how people bullshit each other and, worst of all, themselves. Recently, I hired a man named Willie to do some handyman work for me. He was in his mid-forties, with a long, scraggly beard, which he stroked when he spoke. He was maybe five-feet-six, well over two hundred pounds. He had an inkling that I was in finance and insurance. While working in the backyard, Willie sought my advice. "Mr. Walsh," he said, "I'm not sure what you do for a living, but you probably have health insurance. I keep getting turned down."

I asked him why.

"I don't know," he said. "Nothing's the matter with me."

"Well, Willie, to be honest, I can see you're overweight. So even if you got insurance, it would cost you more than if you weighed less. Do you have any other health issues?"

"Diabetes," he said.

"That's a big one. But it often improves when you lose weight and eat better and get in better shape. How's your cholesterol?"

"My cholesterol?" He practically laughed at the question. "My cholesterol's great!" He smiled. "Since the quadruple bypass."

"You had a quadruple bypass? When?"

"At thirty-five."

"What was the problem?"

"They made me go in for a test. For nothing! Next thing you know, I'm getting bypass surgery."

I nodded. "Dude, you gotta go to the gym," I told him. "You're too young for this."

For some people, heart disease is unavoidable, no matter how healthy a life they live. Still, I found it amazing that Willie—he's not unique in this—could act as if it was almost an afterthought that he had a history of heart disease and other conditions, and that there was little he could do to improve it. He was in disbelief and almost insulted that an insurance company should look at his profile and be wary of covering him.

The lies we tell ourselves.

My angle on the world—hiding in it but being able to look out at it, knowing that likely my biggest challenge was obvious to everyone who gawked at it—is what helped make me, I believe, a quick judge of character, particularly in business. It sharpened my ability to question someone's agenda early on, even as they tried to mask it.

What are they *really* calling me about? Is he *truly* interested in how I'm doing?

Did she look me in the eye? What's their endgame here?

Good poker players possess this skill. So do facial burn survivors.

In the business world, another surefire sign of mask-wearing to be wary of: corporate speak. I dislike it and distrust anyone who uses it as a crutch. To me, those awful catchphrases are a dead giveaway that the user is wearing a mask. They're hiding who they are. Or they're not to be trusted. Or maybe (my number one suspicion) they don't really understand what they're talking about, so they retreat behind a barricade of ridiculous clichés that too many business professionals use.

Let's circle back. I'll ping you. I'm out of pocket. I'm flying at my desk. Action item. (Question: What "item" to achieve a goal *doesn't* require action?) Deliverables. Facetime. Mindshare. Bandwidth. Strat com. Biz meth.

And on and on and on.

Ugh. Who makes this stuff up? I understand these phrases become part of the language, and if everyone talks this way it seems okay to talk like that yourself and assume your listener will get it. But it also means you're saying the same thing everyone else is, because it's easy. It's lazy. If you really thought about what you wanted to say, would you seriously have used *that* phrase? I find that people rarely sprinkle their conversation with just one or two clichés, which seems forgivable; they use them constantly. In the end, it's a sign of inauthenticity. It doesn't reveal who *you* are, which, for me, is at the heart of how another person and I develop a good business relationship. (As for the explanation that using such phrases "saves time": more bullshit. You can say what you want, in your own words, in the same amount of time.) Once, I attended a due diligence meeting for the money manager of a large fund. After a half-hour sitting in the room with five people from the company and hearing them all use nothing but clichés, I thought, *Do they manufacture these people?* They all more or less talked the same, used the same hand gestures, dressed the same, behaved just like the people to their right and left. *Why would you want to be like that?* I thought. *Where is the independent thinking? Where is the individual person beneath all that? Who* *are you?*

That's why I try to have a meal with someone before committing to doing business with them, and why I try not to discuss business over that meal. Breaking bread for the first time with another person is a sacred experience. I want to see how he or she treats our waiter or waitress, the busboy, and everyone else we come in contact with. If it's an upscale restaurant, I want to see if they care where we sit, if it matters to them to be "seen." Are they distracted by factors other than our meeting and connecting? Are they practically grinding their teeth that we're not discussing business even just a tiny bit? I feel the same about golf: if I barely know someone, after the three to four hours it takes to play eighteen holes, I know pretty much everything I need. Did my partner insist on taking a cart? If we have a caddy, did he thank him genuinely and attentively? How did he tip? Did he compete fairly or with a win-at-all-costs mentality? How did he treat his own bad shots? Does he now want to talk business over drinks at the nineteenth hole? (I don't.)

If the new person I dine with or golf with is still wearing a mask through all that, that's not good. Then again, I guess it's not as bad as this alternative: they actually come out from behind the mask only to have me see why they wore one in the first place.

You can't hide. From yourself, sure, sometimes. But usually not *from the rest of us. And in the end, not from yourself either.*

So if you can't hide, don't. If you added up all the "secondary" benefits you jeopardize (e.g., more authentic personal relationships, more expressiveness) by wearing a mask for the "primary" benefits (more business success, creating a persona), you're probably in the red. What's the point?

* * *

I would have given up a lot to not look like I did or have to wear a mask to cover up my reality. A couple of weeks after I left St. Agnes, Jim Noonan asked me to join his family for a weekend at their home right before Christmas. I accepted. I felt close to him. He understood. He had kids my age.

When I met up with him, I was of course wearing my hard-shell mask, and the pressure garment over it. Jim had cleaned, disinfected, and dressed my face at least once a day for a month. Outside of the surgeon—maybe even including him—Jim knew my face better than anyone.

Jim and I drove to a nursery to cut down a Christmas tree for his home. On the way, we talked about this and that, including his kids, Michelle and Sean. We were going more than sixty miles per hour on the expressway, I was in the front seat, and suddenly I was overtaken by a sickening realization.

"Jim, they're looking at me," I said.

"What?" he said. "Who is?"

"The cars coming in the other direction. When they pass. They're staring."

"Brian, there's no way they can see your face at this speed," he said. "No way."

Yet I was sure of it.

When we got to the nursery, I would not exit the car. Part of me really wanted to be out in the winter air, enjoying the physical exertion of cutting down the tree with Jim, and drinking hot cocoa at the little coffee shop next door to the nursery. But I couldn't bring myself to open the car door and get out into the world. There were lots of people milling about. Most of them wore winter hats and hoods, but no one wore something to stop traffic like my mask.

Jim tried his best to convince me to come on out and join him. No one was looking. Everyone was in their own world. I knew he was right. But it wasn't enough. After a few minutes of getting nowhere with me, he let it go.

Self-consciousness is a bitch. I missed an opportunity to have a truly great afternoon with Jim, cutting down a tree and focusing on just him and our bond and the beautiful scenery and other sensory surroundings, walking among the trees and the feel and sound of the crunch of snow, the smell of pine and the cold air and later the hot chocolate, and the taste of whipped cream and the warmth of the cup in my hands. *I experienced none of that available pleasure because I let strangers— strangers!—negatively determine my actions, my emotional state, my happiness.* Because I was too conscious of what was going on—what I thought was going on—in my peripheral vision, I cut out what was right in front of me.

Jim kept the engine running so I would be warm while sitting in the car in the nursery parking lot.

* * *

You can't blame me for that kind of fear. Wanting to hide. My sister Renee said that when she first saw the mask they made for me, she told herself then and there, "He's never leaving the house again, except for doctors' visits." She wasn't wrong to think that. But in February 1982, I was back at Neshaminy High wearing the mask. I was "allowed" to return only to the public high school, not the trade school. Before the accident, I had been studying heating and ventilation at Tech, but now they didn't want me near any explosive material. A little late for that, don't you think? At Neshaminy I also had a restriction: no gym. Why? How was I going to do more damage to my face in gym? Actually, though it was unlikely, a bad cut to the face could now be life-threatening. Still.

Most of my classmates were okay with me on my return and didn't treat me differently. A smaller number weren't. As a rule, the girls adjusted better than the boys. They were kinder to me and generally more normal about it. Terry Bidwell, Barb Murphy, Lenae Rocco—great, all of them. But quite a few guys acted as if I was a different person. Part stranger. Maybe they were scared of the reality of me—not just my face but the living example of me, the fact that a tragedy like that could actually strike a local teen. A little like the fascination with zombies: *What if they walked among us?*

They say you find out your real friends when you go through really tough times, and now I was seeing the truth of that. A guy I'd previously been friendly with wouldn't go to a movie with me. I guess it was just too much for him to be seen with a burn victim. Others were just cruel. One kid, someone I hadn't really known before the fire, muttered as he passed me in the school hallway, "Still have your Halloween mask, I see." Word got back to the Glasson brothers. They beat him up.

I could not understand the mentality of exclusion and mockery. Why would they treat me differently? In my neighborhood we always included a neighborhood boy with cerebral palsy, who walked with difficulty and wore hearing aids in both ears, on any outings where he wanted to join us—amusement park, ballpark, wherever. It wasn't us being nice. It's just what you did.

Most of my closest friends from before the accident were business as usual. It's not as if they pretended that nothing had changed. That would have seemed insincere. But they behaved as if nothing had changed about how they felt about me. I appreciated that. I had to roll with the punches that came with my new life, but they did, too, though in a much less extreme way.

If I expected adults to be more mature and understanding than teens and kids: no. Most of the teachers at my school were fine. Some were neutral—I couldn't tell what they were thinking. But there were quite a few who, whenever we passed in the hall, looked scared to death of me.

I tried not to let it get to me but it did. How could it not? I often cried or wondered if the feeling would ever end.

That wasn't the problem. The problem wasn't the problem. The problem began and ended with me. The crappy feeling could exist only if I allowed it to. *I* had to end it. At some point I had to decide to not let it bother me. Or, rather—though I didn't know it yet—I had to replace being bothered by it, and what it subtracted from me, with bigger, better things that added to me.

* * *

The effect was not on me alone, of course. It was on others, too, and how it made *them* feel, and how I felt about how they felt.

Someone from my father's work had season tickets to Philadelphia Flyers hockey, and he gave Dad a pair for a game in early fall of 1982. It had been almost a year since the fire, and the first heavily populated public event I had attended with my dad since then. My mask looked a lot like the one that Flyers goalie Pelle Lindbergh wore. The seats Dad and I had were excellent, maybe a dozen rows behind the goal.

We didn't even make it to the end of the first period. People kept looking at me. No one said a word, at least not quite loud enough for us to hear, but they were talking about me. You could tell. By this point I was learning to steel myself. Ignore it. I was even teaching myself not to blame people for staring. Who says *I* wouldn't, in their shoes? If you see someone in a mask, are you staring? How about some obvious facial deformity? A person with a prosthetic limb? Even a person in a wheelchair? Yeah, you're looking. I probably would have. Human nature.

At the hockey game my father found all the gawking impossible to ignore. I could see his discomfort growing, though I'm sure he felt it more for me than for himself. I could have been humiliated and heartbroken that he couldn't stand to be out in public with me. But it dawned on me that he must have felt, more than anything, helpless. Here is the son, the object of all this unwanted attention, curiosity, even revulsion, like some freak show, and here is the father, powerless to do a thing about it. But I was still very hurt. Years later, after I became a father, I became more sympathetic to what my dad had been through, as I realized how paralyzed with helplessness you feel when something bad happens to your kid that you didn't prevent and probably couldn't—Brian Jr.'s near-fatal car accident, Matt's diabetes and alcoholism, Katie's hair mysteriously falling out as a pre-teen. In fact, had I been in my father's shoes at the hockey game, I'm pretty sure I would have beaten somebody up. If any one of the Glasson boys had been there with us, there's no question fights would have broken out throughout the Spectrum. I think of the restraint it took for my father not to hit someone. He had to be even more upset about the whole thing than he let on. And shocked by it, too, because why would he ever have taken me to the game if he had any idea of the reaction? Maybe he did expect it but just miscalculated his ability to suffer through it.

* * *

There's some dispute over whose idea it was for me to move down to Memphis and live there for a while with my sister Patty and her family.

I used to visit them for about a week every year, on my own, starting when I was about fourteen. Patty really loved me. She was the one who suggested I be named Brian. We were especially close.

I hadn't thought about leaving home and Levittown to go someplace else, though, until I decided to study fire administration. Two schools offered it: the University of Maryland and Memphis State University. Since I could afford to attend only if I could pay in-state tuition, Patty and the gang were it.

Patty has a slightly different recollection. She told me later that Dad had called and told her, "I'm worried about Brian. He keeps thinking he's going to get better."

"What do you mean by 'get better'?" Patty replied.

"That after all these surgeries, he'll look like he did before," said Dad.

"That's never going to happen," said Patty, who, as a nurse, knew more than most.

"I know, but he keeps thinking that. He doesn't have many scheduled medical appointments for the next couple of months. Can he visit with you for a while?"

I think my account is the more accurate one, but I don't deny that the call occurred.

An unexpected benefit from my time in Patty and Ray's home is that I got to experience a different family dynamic. Growing up in Philly in the house at 14 Quaint Road, I was the youngest; now, at Patty and Ray's, with their two young sons, seven-year-old Chris and four-year-old Danny, I could retire that role, at least for a while. Now I was the oldest, by a lot. There were three "boys" in the home, and I was often left in charge of my nephews. Patty worked long hours as a nurse, and Ray, once an air traffic controller, now worked in personnel. I was not just an extended houseguest but a useful addition to the Bader family. It was usually my job to pick up the boys at daycare and grade school and bring them home, which I did in the Hurst GTO I had driven down there. Chris and Danny had to be the only seven-year-old and four-year-old in the neighborhood getting chauffeured in a muscle car. I gave them their after-school snacks. Other responsibilities included (not all the time) laundry, food shopping, cooking, cutting grass, picking up dry cleaning, and more. It's not what I had gone down south for, but the experience was invaluable for my learning a different kind of responsibility.

I continued to wear the mask all the time, including when I slept. I took it off only when I ate or took a shower. It didn't take long before I stopped even thinking of myself as wearing a mask. Do something long enough and it becomes the norm. The way you had been for years, your whole life previous to that, suddenly becomes the outlier.

I had been in Memphis not even a couple weeks when one night, thirsty for a soda, I walked into a 7-Eleven. The man behind the counter raised his arms. His eyes went wide. I had no idea what was going on.

Then I remembered my mask.

"Oh, my God, wait, wait, no!" I told him. "I'm not robbing you!" It was several seconds before he believed me, and the terrified look in his eyes faded and he finally lowered his arms. I'm very glad he didn't reach for a gun behind the counter.

When I got home, I told Patty and Ray. She shook her head. "God, how cruel people can be."

"People don't know what I've been through. They don't get customers wearing masks. Who wears a mask?"

"Did you get anything?" asked Ray.

"What?"

"Did you get anything when you robbed them?"

God bless Ray for his sense of humor. Or anyone who could joke about it. That helped loosen me up. There's a special place in heaven for those who know how to make light of difficult things, in a way that doesn't deny that it's an actual, tough situation yet also puts it in perspective—the combination of which makes it funny. Soon enough I was saying to Patty and Ray, "Hey, you guys need anything from 7-Eleven? I don't need money. I'll just swing by and see if they remember me."

* * *

Patty and Ray were great to me and for me. If part way through a busy day I felt more exhausted than I thought a healthy eighteen-year-old should, Patty might say, in a kind way, "Hey, Brian, you know what? Unfortunately, that might be a result of the smoke inhalation." I appreciated what she knew and how she communicated it. There was no condescending and no pretending. There was a practicality I found useful. I could learn from her about confronting my situation because I wasn't all the way there yet. How could I be? And my lungs were an ongoing issue. Memphis was a different environment, with a lot more allergens floating in the air than in Philly. But I wanted never to be treated like a sick person. "They said I might have problems with my breathing," I told Patty, letting her know I realized that my life circumstances had changed, at least a little.

I especially loved my time with the boys. Danny, the little one, would pat my masked face and say, "What is that?"

"It's a mask for my scar," I told him. "It's a burn scar. From a burn."

"Mister Burnie," Danny said.

The boys understood me on a different level from how I understood myself. At the time I didn't appreciate it, but *I gradually started seeing myself through their eyes.*

Slowly, very slowly, I became more comfortable with myself than if I had continued to see everything through my eyes only.

* * *

What is it like to have an unfixable face?

My father called Patty with the names of some good plastic surgeons in Memphis. Since Patty at that time worked for a surgeon (though not a plastic surgeon), she asked her boss to look at the list. He recommended someone not on it, Dr. Charles White, who had "a superb reputation." Patty set up an appointment.

When we got there, I removed my mask. I guess his office didn't realize what they were dealing with because when Patty and I announced ourselves at the desk, the first words out of the receptionist's mouth after she laid eyes on me were a startled, "Oh, my."

It's not a great sign when you show up at an office that fixes faces for a living and the staff expresses shock at your appearance.

Patty and I were shown to the inner office. I had with me something I'd brought down to Memphis for just this possibility.

After a few minutes, Dr. White walked in—tall, with salt-and-pepper hair—and we exchanged greetings. I liked his stately, no-nonsense manner. A real gentleman.

"What can I help you with?" he asked, though I figured he already knew the answer.

"I want you to do something with my face," I said.

Dr. White sat up a little straighter. "Well, tell me what you're expecting," he said. "Obviously, you've had some surgeries."

"Yeah, there are lots of scars there," I said. "I don't want all the scars. I want to look better. I want to look like I did before the fire." And then I produced my prop: my high school yearbook. I turned to the page with my graduation photo, taken three weeks before the fire. There was the thick, slightly wavy dark hair. The light eyes, full lips, clear skin, long eyelashes. Pretty handsome dude, I must say. Almost smiling, not quite. Over the previous year, I had looked more than a few times into the eyes of the person in that photograph. He had no clue what was coming.

Dr. White looked at the photo for a few seconds, then up at me. His smile was the serious kind. He closed the book.

"Son, you'll never look like that again," he said.

I don't know how much time passed before I finally spoke again.

"You can't do anything?"

"Son, you'll never look like that again," the doctor repeated. I remember feeling, later, that his repeating the word "son" was the instinct of a naturally kind person.

Eventually, I turned to look over at Patty. She was finding it hard to hold it together.

Neither of us spoke much on the car ride home.

Sometimes you don't know the moment when you actually change, or the crucial spark in a series of moments that finally gets you to a new psychological state. The moment is often hidden. It's small or too bunched up, making it impossible to say *yes, that, there!*—that was the moment.

But sometimes you can. That was a moment, with Dr. White. I don't know about *the* moment. But it was one of several crucial moments in my need to recognize and ultimately accept my situation. The year before, in the bathroom at the end of the hall at St. Agnes, when I stared at the mummy and decided to remove all the bandages to see what it looked like underneath, I cried at the person who looked back. Yet it was not the reckoning that this was. That was way too early. It was always in my mind or my heart that I was fixable, practically reversible. *This is not permanent*, I convinced myself. But now, a top plastic surgeon, someone with a great reputation in the field and who I could see for myself was naturally empathetic: now *that* guy was telling me, no bullshit—twice!—that what I wanted was not going to happen.

Would never happen.

In the silent car ride home with Patty, I could have said something like, "Screw it, I give up." It's not like I didn't consider that option. I knew from John, my social worker, about the difficulty many people in situations like mine had, just giving up psychologically. And how, once you do that, all kinds of things start going wrong.

But it was a fleeting thought. It wasn't me. Weeks after I left the burn center, Jim Noonan had told me about the exchange he had with John, and John's dire psychological profile of me. *Thank you very much for thinking I **should** be suicidal*, I had thought, *but I'm not going anywhere*. I had laughed and so had Jim. "He doesn't know you," Jim said at the time.

Now, a year later, if I was being totally honest, I had to admit that I knew in my heart the answer before I set foot in Dr. White's office. I knew it before I stuffed my high school yearbook in the duffel I was taking to Memphis. I wasn't generally the kind of person to delude himself. I knew that I was carrying around a delusion, but I allowed it because it was necessary to steel myself against the truth. Then I sort of forgot for a while that it was, in the end, a delusion I had nurtured. But when I sat there in Dr. White's office and opened the yearbook to that photograph of Brian Patrick Walsh, I pretty much knew that that guy was dead, even if I would never say it. The original physical version of me was gone.

Why did I make a scene? Because I had to live for a little while with the plain truth of what I now looked like before I could accept it and get past it. I held that moment off until there was simply too much evidence to ignore. I didn't have a next, positive place to get to yet, something that I believed in and was excited about, which would focus me and allow me to discard the delusion.

It was a moment for Dr. White, too. I could see it in his face, which is why I knew how final it was.

In fact, the kindness of Dr. White in that meeting really helped, more than he ever knew. I could see how hard it was for him, an expert in messed-up faces, to speak the truth to me. I could see the moment hit him. To have that kind of humanity surrounding me—him, my sister and her family, my parents and the rest of my family up in Philadelphia, my friends who kept with me, strangers who showed me kindnesses— that sounded like a life worth living. Or at least important pieces of one.

As much as you think you're being honest with yourself, I learned, you often need someone to do the honesty for you, to give you perspective, to put it in their words or give you a penetrating look that you know speaks the truth. For this reckoning to work, that someone has to be a person you respect or trust. Four-year-old Danny did it for me by nicknaming me Mr. Burnie. Dr. White did it for me with his words, his eyes, his expertise and reputation. On the car ride home with Patty, I began to understand: *the brutally honest inner conversations we have with ourselves go only so far before they get warped by lack of objectivity or a desire to minimize the pain, or because the person on both sides of the dialogue is just not yet old enough or wise enough.*

Thanks to Dr. White, I needed to keep telling myself: *This is what I look like now. This is pretty much what I will look like, period.*

It was time to turn the page.

* * *

"Nick's biggest problem," Terry Saban said of her football coach husband, "is he doesn't know how other people view him."

As I wrote at the start of this chapter, I didn't buy that comment at first, for a couple of reasons. But then I realized that *for another person to know you requires that you share who you really are with them (duh), so they have a chance to see the real you.* Which means *you* must know the real you, and you aren't hiding behind a mask because masks make you appear different to others, as well as making it harder for you to know yourself.

Some may disagree with the "wisdom" that it's good to know what others think of us. Who wants the hassle of worrying about other people's opinions? But I believe most of us *do* want to know, or maybe need to know, because we ultimately benefit by knowing.

I don't suggest going through something like I did. But my misfortune afforded me the "gift" of seeing how other people truly viewed me, at least initially. It forced me to be honest about how I looked and how I was perceived by a lot of the world, and steeled me to come up with a plan to do something about it, all at a fairly young age. If you're lucky enough to live a long life, most people eventually get to a certain point of understanding. Circumstances force some people to that point sooner than others. A great misfortune, right? "Grew up quickly" is always said as if it's a negative.

For me, it was not. It made me comfortable early on with honesty. It prepared me better to deal with people. Once upon a time I wore a mask, an actual mask. I don't wear one anymore, literal or metaphorical. I never do. I don't have to. This is who I am. Confronting myself comes easier than it probably does for a lot of people.

Except for the night of Halloween and the once-in-a-blue-moon costume ball, any mask-wearing is a waste of your time, time you're never getting back to be your real self.

* * *

In the years since the fire, I count between forty-four and forty-six operations. My left eyelid alone has been operated on five times. The skin now on the lid—the muscle still functions—was taken from behind my ear and my thigh, which explains the patchy pigmentation. Corneal ulcers, brought about by complications from the burning around my eyes, sent me to the ER for years; not only were they extremely painful but if not treated immediately and they popped or got infected, I could have lost my sight within twenty-four hours. (Hard to believe but true: The ultimate cause of the ulcers, finally discovered by my brother-in-law Frank the Ophthalmologist, was ingrown eyelashes.)

I've had five surgeries on my upper lip. It would have been four, but while I was healing in the hospital from the fourth, my father visited me and told me a joke he never should have, and I couldn't help but literally bust out laughing, causing the stitches in my lip to rip apart and a fountain of blood to gush forth. I was not happy. The surgeon was *really* not happy. My dad hid somewhere in the hospital because he was so distraught and terrified of the surgeon's wrath.

I've had five "z-plasties," where the skin on my neck got so tight that I couldn't turn my head, so they cut a *Z* just under the back of the jawline and grafted extra skin over the incision to open things up. I'll be honest, it looks cooler on Zorro.

There are all kinds of things that we do to ourselves—masks or airs we put on—or that people do to us—surgeries, for example—to make us appear less broken. In the end, our greatest asset may be the pride we take in being broken without letting it break us.

CHAPTER 4:

Look in the Mirror

Get busy living or get busy dying.
—"Red" Redding (Morgan Freeman),
The Shawshank Redemption

What drives you?

What's the thing you're trying to do while you're here? Thrive or survive? Do you want success for you, do you want it for others, or do you feel as if achieving one is achieving the other and it's all intertwined? Have you ever defined what "success" would feel like when you achieved it?

We all have an innate desire to live. But do we all have an innate desire to succeed? We all have an instinct to avoid loss. But do we have the will and imagination to turn loss into gain?

You can die without physically dying.

When you go through something terrible, you don't have the option of whether or not to grapple with these ideas, of whether you need to bother really looking at yourself in the mirror. How hard did I have to work before people saw me as recovered? Before I saw myself as recovered? If I got to 50 percent of the potential I had before the fire, would that be a huge success and moral victory, end of story? What if it was only 10 percent? If I worked my ass off to make something of my life, and still failed...would I get "credit" for a superhuman effort? Would that admiration matter one bit, if failure was still the verdict? And how was I defining success and failure? *Hey: You're a burn victim wearing a mask and a mouth stretcher, living in your parents' house. Who would blame you if the only time you ventured outside was for doctor visits? Or if you decided to get a job with a low profile, low ceiling, and little interaction with others?*

For a while after the fire, I didn't bother to ask myself what motivated me. I was going from one point to the next, one facial surgery to the next, trying to steal pockets of peace, reasons for hope, a bit of normalcy, which was hard to find when I was out in public. I had no external pressure to assert myself. No one would dare show disappointment in me when my life had taken such an unfortunate turn through no real fault of my own. I could have been a shut-in, dreaming of a life I might have had but now clearly wouldn't. There's a seductive comfort in lower expectations, even if it's an empty comfort. It would take so much more effort to figure out how to live the best real-life life I could.

With all that built-in inertia, I'm glad there were motivations I could use or even manufacture to push me. Showing up the doubters, for example. Some people seemed almost as if they wanted me to fail, perhaps because they themselves didn't want to be left behind. Proving them wrong about me or about "burn victims" or about the possibilities of life in general could be a strong motivator.

How about reaffirming the faith of those who believed in me? That was another powerful incentive.

At some point, though, and I can't say exactly when or why, I was driven by an awareness of legacy, of an epitaph. Whoever I matured to be, I wanted the phrase, "That's Brian," to mean something positive, something that made others happy. I couldn't stop "Burn Guy" from being the first thought that new people had about me, but I could make it not be the last. The more good qualities I became known for, the less room there would be for Burn Guy, even as Burn Guy had motivated my developing some of those qualities.

What virtues would "That's Brian" imply? For one, I wanted to be able to see the truth. My eyes had been literally closed and my vision blurred for long enough, that I had come to prize clarity. If I was going to shoot straight with people and myself, I needed to know the score.

I wanted to use whatever intelligence I had, whatever street smarts, whatever common sense and resources, to get the most out of myself. I might not have been the smartest person in the room, but it was within my power to outwork whoever was. (I thought of that line, "You know why God made C students? So that A and B students have someone to work for.")

I wanted "That's Brian" to mean someone who got things done. I wanted to be the one to come up with a solution, not just identify a problem. Better yet, I wanted to be the one to implement the solution.

I wanted "That's Brian" to mean someone who really listened, which also meant being capable of change. That alone would probably make me stand out.

In the end, though, if I wanted to make "That's Brian" really stand out, I couldn't make it about Brian. (Sorry for talking about myself in the third person.) I had to make it about others, for others. After all, *they* would be the ones using the phrase, not me.

* * *

I caution my kids, my friends, myself: when you're in a room and you're looking around for the idiot and you can't find him, it's probably you.

I don't think that they're idiots, or that I am. It's just my reminder that we all have blind spots that, by definition, we don't immediately recognize. It's another reason to look in the mirror.

Anyone who operates in a dangerous situation is wary of what they don't see, can't see. I *don't* look to the night of the fire as an example of how blind spots can lead to one's downfall. I didn't have my breathing apparatus on me because I was not expected to enter the burning building, and even more experienced firefighters attached it to their gear only when they were about to go in. I entered the burning building because I was asked, it was needed, and there was no one else to help get the hose up to the third floor, then and there. I scouted for "extension of fire" because, again, I was asked, I was the body right there, and we didn't yet know that a highly unusual occurrence, a flashover, was imminent.

Still, all the little decisions that precede such a life-changing event, all the little things that aren't known or understood until after the fact, can haunt you, at least in the days and weeks and months and even couple of years after (and, for some people, until the day they die). What you could have done, what you should have done. I once heard a motivational speaker say, "We're always, 'I should have done this, I should have done that, I should have done this...,' It's time to stop shoulding all over yourself!"

I have made it a point to not be the last to identify my shortcomings. Everyone's got blind spots, but it's a thousand times easier to see them in others. CEOs have blind spots, everything from how they could sometimes deal better with people to being overly focused on the short-term. Rich people have blind spots, often in how they think that throwing money at a problem is always the solution. Smart, successful people have blind spots in the way they can convince themselves that their previous success guarantees that their next idea or utterance is infused with similar brilliance. Clients of mine have blind spots, often in how they let emotion cloud their judgment, costing themselves lots of money.

I try to assess myself the way I would someone else. I recognize many of my faults. For example, I can revert to worst-case scenario right away. I'm not good at spur-of-the-moment. I'm stubborn. I'm a creature of habit, whether it's watching *Law & Order* episodes over and over when I can't sleep or going back to the same restaurant and constantly ordering the same dish. (Seriously, though: Why change when you've got a good thing going?) I can get mad for all kinds of reasons. I'm blunt, often way too much. I obsess about righting wrongs in a way that's sometimes not productive. This is hardly a complete list.

I don't kill myself over my shortcomings, though. I want to be conscious of them, all of them, and sooner rather than later. I want to fix those that I can. But many of them, probably most, I won't be able to fix. And that's where the danger comes in: If I know them, and I know

I can't fix them, I might just become complacent about them. I think of the mask I wore for two years: it became a part of me, but I never let it become me. I accepted it but I never totally got used to it.

When you look in the mirror, really look. If you're just glancing, don't waste your time (or the reflection's).

*   *   *

Several years after the fire I got a call from someone at St. Agnes asking if I would mentor a patient, same age as me, once he "graduated" from the burn unit—visit him and his loved ones at their home, maybe give them an idea of what lay ahead. Frank had been filling a propane tank at the gas station when the tank exploded. He suffered bad burns on his torso, not his face. Not that I'm minimizing that. You don't want to be burned anywhere. I don't care if it's your pinky toe.

Frank was still living in his childhood home. His father had passed away a few years earlier, so it was just him and his mother. I sat first with Frank's mom, heard the things she was struggling with. The difficulty of the situation was compounded by the fact that, before the accident, Frank had some cognitive issues—I'm not sure the best way to describe them except to say he had challenges both mental and social.

With each visit and call, Frank grew more attached to me. He called frequently. The people at the burn center told me that this was common and I would need to try to help him while also keeping my distance. Easier said than done.

I came to consider him a pal. I tried to "separate," for my sake as much as his. I didn't think it was great for him to define himself too much by his association with me. But maybe that was my own bias, my own strength and weakness. I had been working hard to transcend my life's defining moment, to the point that others would not ridicule or label or even notice me (ha!) because of it. Frank and I would talk on the phone. Now and then, we would get together. His mom passed away. He moved in with his sister. I would check in. He continued to call, but more sporadically. I wanted Frank to be master of his life, much as I tried to be of mine. But while some circumstances are very obviously in our control, and some seem as if they're not but really are, some truly aren't.

Frank made me realize how lucky I was. There were assets I had that he simply didn't. Luck of the draw. Since the fire, I had silently compared myself to the rest of the world, the non-burned world. When I met Frank, a fellow burn "victim," I couldn't help but compare myself to him, too, and see where I stood. And that's what made me realize, *No, you're not behind everyone who isn't burned. Everyone's got troubles. Everyone's got advantages.*

In the mask I was the least anonymous person in any crowd. I was also the most. That forced me to have to identify myself *to* myself. Not everyone has to do that.

So I made it my aim always to look in the mirror and be honest about what I saw.

Okay, your path got blocked…now what? Give up?

Is this the way you want to live?

If not, then how do you want to live?

Who are you?

For me, it meant involving myself more and more in all the conversations about my treatment, the decisions being made, the choice of medications. I immersed myself in the evaluation of doctors and the scheduling of procedures. My parents were very involved, but I made an effort not to be in the dark about anything. "That's Brian" would mean someone who took charge. I knew that if I was going to recover, then I had to be all in, and do what the doctors and physical therapists told me to do, all the way, the best way I knew how, and maybe even then some. I wanted an actual life, not just to keep living. *I would follow the rules and, for good measure, I would torque it up a notch, to get the best possible result, not just a result.* Later on, this would be a great mindset for trying to get ahead in my chosen profession. For now, though, it was about my recovery. I didn't want plain old recovery. I wanted exceptional recovery.

I wanted to be the exception.

Since the months after my accident, when I was in my late teens, I have had no choice but to look in the mirror. If I didn't face everything head on, I would have had no life.

Looking in the mirror, and meeting that person's gaze head on, is a reckoning. Sure, you can look away. *You can avoid the mirror altogether. Just know that by doing that, you're choosing to know less about your capabilities and shortcomings than if you really looked. You're choosing to have less control of the legacy you're trying to shape.*

Look. Really look.

CHAPTER 5:

Trust What You See, Not What Others See in You

I'm not in this world to live up to your expectations
and you're not in this world to live up to mine.
—Bruce Lee

As a parent it's hard not to pick a path for your kid. It's hard for a loved one not to think they know better. Growing up I learned that authority was not to be questioned. If I came home after school and told my parents, good Roman Catholics that they were, that Sister Saint Angela had hit me, mine was not the side they were taking. They assumed I had done something to deserve the nun's wrath. She was the Church, I merely the student. When I was in the hospital after the fire, anything that came out of a doctor's mouth was considered gospel, never mind that doctors often disagree with one another. I'm not saying the doctors were wrong—just that my parents believed they couldn't be. Their logic: some people just know what's better for you. Which is often true.

And often not.

Take my first real "career choice," post-accident. I was twenty years old, living at home, still going to regular doctors' appointments and getting more skin grafts, and I thought I wanted to be a fire inspector for the Federal Emergency Management Agency (FEMA), the first step to being a FEMA fire marshal, the position I was really aiming for. Everyone thought it was an obvious path for me—that is, for someone who looked like I now looked. I applied. I received a letter that I was wait-listed.

In the meantime, I needed a job. In the classified section of our local newspaper, I saw an ad for an internship with Mutual of Omaha, the insurance company, in Willow Grove, a suburb north of Philadelphia. I had never thought about insurance as a profession or even a temp job. I applied and got called in for an interview. I thought it went well but they didn't hire me. I assumed many candidates had seen the ad and some were more qualified. I didn't kid myself that I was some slam-dunk.

I continued to search the classifieds and spotted an ad for another Mutual of Omaha internship, this time in Bensalem, a fifteen-minute drive from Levittown. During the interview with the office manager, Joe Marino, who was just getting his feet wet after running another office, we completely hit it off. We talked about our backgrounds. He mentioned that he had been a volunteer firefighter. Then he asked, "How'd you get burned?"

I told him.

I reminded him that this was actually my second Mutual of Omaha face-to-face.

"Yeah, I know," said Joe. "You interviewed at Willow Grove. It's in our records. The guy who interviewed you there told me you did very well."

"Really? I didn't get an offer."

"He was never gonna hire you."

"What? Why?"

"He said you would never succeed in a face-to-face business like insurance," said Joe. But before I could get upset or righteous, he said, "*I'll* give you a shot. I don't know anyone who went through anything like you did. I'm amazed you're sitting across from me. I love your attitude."

I appreciated Joe's candor and especially the opportunity he was giving me. I did not appreciate the Willow Grove manager making assumptions about my capabilities, which was the same narrow, limiting judgment that the therapist at the burn center had made about my future.

Six months into the Bensalem internship, a letter from FEMA arrived at home: there was a job opening for fire inspector. I was to report to Willow Grove Naval Air Station to claim my $14,300-a-year government position (about $34,000 today). Everybody in my family was thrilled.

"I'm going to be a life insurance agent," I told my parents and friends.

I appreciated what my circle wanted for me. They meant well. But they all had only modest expectations for me professionally, maybe personally, too. (Not my wife: Mary Ann believed fully in me from the start.) Their view of my future—my boss Joe was an exception—did not seem to include fulfilling dreams. Or maybe bothering even to have them.

My foregoing the security of a government job made them nervous for my future. A number of them may even have been disappointed in me, expecting I should have had enough common sense to recognize a good thing when it landed in my lap, especially after the terrible thing that had happened. *Life is a crapshoot, Brian, you know that now as well as anyone…and look! You just got a Get Out of Jail Free card! Lucky son of a gun!*

I could almost hear what they *weren't* saying, similar to what the Willow Grove office manager had been thinking.

Are you sure this is the best career path for you?

To be a successful insurance agent, you have to do face-to-face visits—you know that, right?

Cold-calling is tough enough—you really want to do this thing?

I did. I understood. It's not as if I hadn't thought about it in the months I had been working for Mutual of Omaha. It's not as if I hadn't thought about it when I first heard that an experienced insurance professional had rejected me because he thought my face was a business liability. Yeah, I got it: How would a potential client react, after we had spoken by phone and made an appointment to meet at their home, when they opened the door…and saw *me*? You never want to make the customer uncomfortable, especially one who isn't yet your customer. There would definitely be A Moment, a sizing up that was different and more jarring than the usual one between salesperson and customer.

That's what I thought everyone was thinking about me and my so-far-imaginary insurance career. In this new industry, the very issue I had hoped to get past—*What happened to YOU?*—would be the unavoidable topic, even if no one said anything. What kind of way is that to conduct business?

Were they right? Was I naïve to think I could just forge ahead? Wasn't it true that potential clients would have trouble judging me based just on the quality of my performance?

I had to know for myself. And I had something going in my favor. The whole issue everyone was concerned about—how I would be perceived—was not an automatic dead end. It was actually a two-way street, and that could be a good thing. My "condition" wasn't something only *I* had to overcome. The other person—the imaginary client I was meeting for the first time—did, too. I thought of how John, the social worker, had visited my high school while I was still in the hospital, preparing my classmates and teachers for me, as much as I had to prepare for them. If there was going to be a deep bond between client and agent, then we both had distance to cover. In some ways, my scarred face could work to my benefit. When a potential client—or anyone, really—first laid eyes on me, they could see right away that there was a story to tell, probably a powerful, emotional story. (In a way, my face looking the way it did had worked *for* me getting the Bensalem internship, right after it had worked *against* me with the Willow Grove internship.) My face told a story that was more uplifting than depressing. Because here I was, in front of them, doing something productive, aspiring to something greater. Trying to turn a dream into reality. Not hiding. And in a very obvious way, my story was perfect for explaining the importance of insurance. Here I was, giving my future client credit for having the character to see past what they were looking at. I wasn't exploiting my situation. I never referred to it as a tragedy. But it wasn't hard to see how it could be an advantage, at least with open-minded, kindhearted people (which I believe describes the majority). With every doorbell I rang, I had an opportunity to address and normalize my situation. In that initial moment, when they first laid eyes on this stranger, they couldn't escape me or reject me, and I was pretty sure they wouldn't. I had faith in people. They would invite me in, where it would then be up to me, with all my skills as a person, salesman, and young insurance agent to close the deal.

And if they seemed uncomfortable—and even if they didn't—I would be upfront. "If you find it difficult to deal with me," I would tell them, "I'm not offended, I promise you. I understand I look very different from anyone you have probably ever seen. Even some people in my family find it difficult to look at me. They'd never known a burn survivor before me. I can get someone else in our office to follow up with you."

In some ways, building relationships might be *easier* for me.

If I had avoided an exciting professional and life opportunity because it required that I make regular face-to-face visits, what would that say about me, every hour of every day? That I had something to be ashamed about. That I was scared because I was scarred. That certain doors just weren't open to me because…why? Because *other* people, from strangers even to people who loved me, thought so. I remembered how I had once sat hiding in Jim Noonan's car, refusing to go out into the beautiful winter day to cut down a Christmas tree with him, depriving myself of an experience I really wanted because of my fear that strangers might stare at me.

Once I saw my face as a potential asset, not some massive deficit, I thought, *Maybe it takes guts to do what I'm doing. Maybe the people I interact with will admire me for what I'm doing, the way Joe Marino had.* Standing before them was someone who knew a thing or two about overcoming obstacles. This insurance salesman, who wanted them to believe he was the best person to sell to them and manage something so personal, had to grow as a human being himself. He must have some decent traits, this Brian Walsh guy. Perseverance, humility, a rock-solid belief in himself.

It struck me that I was asking the customer to do exactly what any good salesperson asks of him or herself: see things from the other side. If a good salesperson sees things from the customer's side, then I just wanted the person across from me to see things from mine.

Of course, there was more to it than just me being some stand-up guy worthy of respect because he had gone through a visibly harrowing experience. I had to be good at the job. I would make them remember me for the right reasons, for the quality of my performance.

When I considered the response to my turning down the FEMA job offer, part of me was scared, sure, thinking, *Am I an idiot, making a huge mistake?* But it was quickly overtaken by the thought, *This is my life. You guys go ahead and choose what's best for* your *life.* **I was the only one who could live the life I was given**—the life I had almost lost several times within a few short weeks when I was seventeen. Like everyone, I had to live with any decision I made. But I wanted to make sure it was *my* decision.

I wonder if I felt confidence in my decision-making because I was the only one in my circle whose perspective on this I could really trust. I knew zero people at the time with a face like mine. That's a lesson right there: **if your position is unique, then maybe don't bother listening to people who think they're so wise when their experience of the world is so different.**

By day I worked, by night I studied for my insurance certification exam. I was twenty-one, living in my childhood home in Levittown, basically just my mother and me: the older siblings were long gone from the house—I finally had the upstairs room all to myself—and my father now worked for a company based in Williamsport, three-plus hours away, so he was home mostly only on weekends. When I wasn't working or studying, or my friends weren't working or going to school, we'd hang out—the Glassons, Tom Stewart, Mike and Mark Smith, Mike Murtha—and play street hockey or basketball or watch sports. This was the era when all four major Philadelphia teams—the Eagles, Flyers, Phillies, and 76ers—were really good, so it was lots of fun. Villanova University, whose campus was forty-five minutes from my house, had recently upset Georgetown for the national championship in one of the greatest college basketball games ever played, and everyone from the neighborhood poured into the streets that night, banging pots in celebration.

After I passed the licensing test, I could officially pursue what I enjoyed and believed I would be good at. Choosing insurance as a field, at least for the time being, and sticking with it over a safer option, was more than just a great career decision. It felt liberating, intoxicating. By going down that path, I felt much less fear about trying new situations. I felt less fear and concern about what people would think of me, or *could* think of me.

It's easy to say something like "Believe in yourself." I have a different approach, an actual exercise: *Make a list of all the people who believe in you, with all your many capabilities and talents. Are you—you, yourself—number one on the list? At least in the top five? (Parents, grandparents, and best friends might crowd you out.) If not, then something's wrong. Something needs fixing.*

* * *

So many people around me were banking on a different reality.

My father and brother took me to lunch at Steak and Ale. I didn't realize it was more intervention than lunch. They tried to talk me into taking the FEMA job, and not going into insurance. They thought people wouldn't be kind to me. They thought I should look at reality; basically, look in the mirror. I understood that they believed they were doing the loving thing.

It's not that they wanted me to fail, of course. But they expected me to. They had already told themselves a pretty credible story of my failure. They had rationalized why someone in my situation might fail. I'm sure for some people around me, it was a done deal.

But it was always *their* reality. It's not that they didn't love me. They did, and they thought, rightly so, that they were protecting me from lots of rejection, failure, and heartache. But their reality—what they imagined a person would feel and would be unable to achieve in the aftermath of such a calamity—did not allow for real success. In a way, I wasn't even offended that they were pre-judging me. I think they were pre-judging *anyone whose face has third-degree burns over its entirety*. They were discounting me, the individual. They acted as if the equation of

My Present Condition + Excessive Public Face Time =
Miserable Failure

was as true as 2 + 2 = 4. But an individual can rise above his or her circumstances. It was tough having people lecture me about how things would or should play out when I was the only one any of us knew with this particular handicap.

Look: unless 100 percent of people behave the same way in a set of circumstances, there's *always* someone who will act differently. At one point, more than 90 percent of the patients in the St. Agnes burn unit died from infection caused by the silent spread of pseudomonas. I was the lone survivor. I beat the odds. By a lot. Maybe it wasn't totally random. Maybe I was helped by my relative youth and vitality. Maybe if I had been forty years old, I would never have walked out of that unit. And twelve out of twelve would have died.

But that's not what happened. It can be dangerous to generalize.

It's easier to accept lower expectations in yourself—by others and by you. *So* much easier. Less work, less hassle, less energy to expend. But doing that means you're buying into other people's realities rather than testing what you're capable of in your own.

Yeah, no thanks. I'd been dead already.

* * *

Risk.

What does the word mean to you? I'm sure there are people who assume, when they hear about my accident, that I courted risk. Who assume that any firefighter, and certainly a teenage volunteer firefighter who loved cars and driving fast (and still loves cars and driving fast, though not quite as fast), is a risk-taker.

I honestly don't know what the word "risk" means. I'm not kidding. This is not a dyslexic thing. Technically, yes, I understand what the word means. But if you really think about it, what does it mean?

I believe there is no such thing as risk, as we commonly interpret the word. There is living right and well, and living stupidly. Maybe when people say "risk," they really mean "carelessness" or "recklessness." But those are very different ideas. Those words mean doing something by following a bad plan, or following no plan, or lacking awareness that a plan might be useful. Or refusing to consider that things may not turn out as you hope. Pretty much any activity, from eating to exercising to investing to drinking to job-switching to getting married to having kids to not getting married to not having kids—they all have a range of outcomes, desired and undesired. Isn't there risk in simply engaging in that activity? Or does it become risky only if you engage carelessly and even blindly?

In my business life, now more than a quarter-century's worth, I don't feel as if I have ever failed, though at times I've lost money or deals didn't work out. I don't think that's just a semantic point, so that I can say, "I never failed." I mean that I don't take risks—good risks, bad risks, any kind of risk. (I realize that people who do things that I do sometimes call themselves "risk managers.") I make educated choices. Would I do certain things differently, after the fact? Hell yeah! Could certain situations have worked out better? Absolutely! But I never feel I've taken a known risk that ended badly. No. It just didn't end as well as I had hoped. I accounted for the eventual outcome, though. By planning for the range of outcomes, I mitigated their capacity to sting.

This is an occasion where business wisdom and life wisdom are basically the same: *If you believe in yourself—your effort, your attention to detail, your integrity, your ultimate goals—then there's zero risk involved in how you live your life*. There's a peace of mind we're all after.

By "risk," maybe we mean engaging in some act whose outcome we can't possibly know, bad *or* good. That seems like a more accurate definition (though it also applies to pretty much everything). So when I look back, sure, I did take risks, lots of them, like everyone does. I risked it when I went into that building, though I didn't feel as if I had a choice. What awaited me was a total unknown, and not something I could fully prepare for. Maybe I took a risk when I moved to Memphis to live with Patty and Ray and the boys. I risked it when I turned down the FEMA job. I risked it when I asked Mary Ann to lunch soon after we met. And on and on. With all these decisions, I didn't know where I would land. That's life. But in each case, I was at the center of it, and I had the power to affect the outcome—if not completely, then a really good chunk of it. And since I have more belief in myself than I do in other people, I always liked my odds.

Basically: *If you're not betting on yourself all the time, you're just gambling.*

We take different risks than others do because we're different and because we're all betting on someone different: ourselves. My threshold for unacceptable risk is different from yours. Just make sure the threshold you use is yours, not someone else's. My friend Kevin Glasson had the chance to purchase a plumbing company, and given his family's financial situation, he took it (though at first it wasn't what he was dreaming about). He spent six grand to buy the seller's van, tools, and contacts, and proceeded to build a profitable, solid company, exceeding the success of the previous owner, as he expanded to include installing boilers, baseboard heat, and air-conditioning systems. The business wasn't for me—early on Kevin asked if I wanted to go in with him—but I was impressed enough by his belief in himself that I started imagining how one day I would open my own business, too.

In 1991, I took out a home equity loan and, with a friend, rented an office roughly one hundred fifty square feet, just big enough to hold a desk, chair, and filing cabinet. I had clients from my time at Mass Mutual, a big insurance company. (I didn't have to sign a non-compete when I left.) A friend who took care of my car insurance gave me other leads. He'd say, "Hey, I was seeing so-and-so for their commercial insurance and they need a group health plan" or "They need a 401k," something like that, and he would give me their number.

If I was going to bet on one person, it was going to be me.

* * *

There's a system in place when something happens like it did to me. Whether you like it or not, you have to play certain games, follow certain conventions.

When the insurer for my township balked at covering my medical and hospital costs from the accident because I was underage, my parents and I filed a lawsuit. After lots of back and forth, we won. They would cover the expenses. As part of the settlement, I had to agree to a "medical evaluation" by a doctor in New York City. I assumed they meant an internist, a surgeon, a pulmonary specialist, maybe someone who specialized in dermatology, to evaluate and corroborate my physical injuries. I took the train up with Jim, a paralegal from the law firm we had worked with to recover the insurance money. It was unclear to me why I needed to be accompanied for what was a simple visit to the doctor. And why New York? It's not like Philly had no good doctors.

When I got to a Dr. MacGregor's office at the hospital, she asked me about the fire, my reaction to it, and the aftermath. I answered matter-of-factly. Then she handed me a pen and paper.

"I'd like you to draw a picture of yourself walking a dog," she said.

"Excuse me?"

"Just do the best you can."

Okay.

She was a shrink. I had been punked. I wanted to get out of there as soon as possible, so I played along. Since I'm no artist, I drew a stick figure of a man, a fire hydrant, and a dog taking a leak. The dog looked unusually aggressive, I admit. I turned the drawing to her. I felt like a little kid.

She studied it. "Why do you have the dog urinating on the hydrant?" she asked.

"I can't tell you why," I said, "because it's the neighbor's dog."

She asked me to draw a few other things—my family, the firehouse, the building I had been trapped in. I was now actively messing with her and giving smartass answers because I was so pissed at everyone playing me for a fool. My pictures were bizarre and angry. I thought it was from my being upset with the doctor and the situation, and mad at the law firm for misleading me. For a moment I wondered and worried if my drawing of an angry dog—and, weirdly, not *my* dog—gave the shrink enough evidence to recommend I be put away.

Eventually, she asked me, "How do you feel walking around in this mask?"

"Great," I said. "I love it. Nobody sees me. I see the world through a completely different lens from anyone else. It fits me. Yeah. That's kind of where I'm at with it."

She was getting nothing out of me. By now you probably realize that I wasn't a big dump-out-all-your-feelings guy, at least not then.

She nodded. "Okay," she said. "Let's take a fifteen-minute break."

Out in the waiting room, Jim, my handler, was flipping through a magazine. Mr. Innocent.

"We're done," I said.

"Yeah? Already?"

"Yep, done."

I walked briskly out of the office, Jim half-running to keep up, heading to Penn Station. I don't know that I've ever been that angry in my life. I felt insulted. I felt as if control of my life—judgment of it, with the power to then act on it—was being handed to someone else. At the train station Jim found a payphone to call the home office. After a brief exchange, he turned to me. They must have gotten a call from the shrink that I had left her office prematurely.

"They want to know how it went," said Jim.

"Yeah, tell them if they ever send me to a goddamn meeting like that again, I'll kill someone."

After Jim hung up the phone, he asked me, "What happened in there?"

"Don't worry about it," I said.

On the train, I told Jim I wanted to grab a beer in the café car. "I'll be back in a few," I said quickly, not giving him a chance to invite himself along.

I sat in the café car, drinking and getting angrier. At the Trenton stop, I slipped off the train, found a payphone, and called Kevin Glasson. I told him to come get me. It was a long story.

Poor Jim didn't realize that I had ditched him. When he got back to 30th Street Station in Philly, he was beside himself with panic. When he returned to the law office, he told them simply, "I lost Brian Walsh."

Later, when they got hold of me, I told them, "Never put Jim in my sight again, I swear to God."

And right there was a lesson I would not really learn for many years: *You can actually believe in yourself to a degree that's harmful.* Don't get me wrong: I had reason to be wary of anyone who thought they knew better than I what would work for me, in my circumstance. After all, I had once had a smooth-skinned therapist tell me confidently that I would never work anywhere with people, and a non-disfigured nun ask me to thank God for all my pain and suffering. There was that. None of the people dispensing advice were the ones walking around looking like this; *I* was. So I believed I had to be right. Because no one was qualified to tell me I was wrong.

Which only showed that maybe I *did* need to speak to someone like Dr. MacGregor and hear her out. And poor Jim was only doing his job.

At that moment, though, there was only one person in my camp who was 100 percent utterly believable and trustable: me.

* * *

As I focused more on what I wanted to achieve rather than what had befallen me, I glimpsed what success could look like. None of it relied on what I looked like. One of the subtle but important shifts that occurred back when I lived in Memphis at Patty and Ray's was that I started truly to take charge of what was going on. I started to feel as if there wasn't anything I couldn't do, as long as there was a map.

Back then, I had enrolled at Memphis State University's Fire Academy, to get an administrative degree in the field of fire protection. I wanted to continue with firefighting, or thought I did. I enjoyed the classes, sort of. In the evening, I would sometimes talk with Patty about what I had learned—cool stuff but different from what I thought it would be.

I was quietly, purposefully moving toward something else, something new, though I didn't know it yet. I want to say I was shedding my old skin. I was coming to understand my situation—that this was how it was going to be for the rest of my life and I had to up my game. Patty and Ray could see an evolution happening in me. They claimed, later, that they could see the turn: *He's putting It behind him.* But could they really see that? Maybe it's like parents who can't recognize that their child has grown taller because they see him day after day, then one day they just notice this giant in their house.

It wasn't that I would never again think about the accident and its aftermath—that wasn't an option—but I was starting to find a way to mold my life around them, not be exclusively defined by them. Inching forward to become a full grown-up.

Toward the end of my second semester at Memphis State, I realized I didn't want to continue down that exact path. It didn't nourish me. The expectations of others meant nothing to me. The only expectations to consider were mine, and they were big. Ignoring the expectations of others meant no limits. It meant freedom. And ***having expectations of my own didn't mean pressure; it meant purpose.*** I looked unique, so why not live a unique life? Why not be myself? Maybe my "weakness" could be a strength, a springboard, because it would help me to learn and grow and push more than if I didn't possess that weakness/strength. If I lived an honest, non-deluded life, and if I believed in myself, was there really any obstacle that was insurmountable?

It made me think about what I would have been like had I never been in that fire, what it was like for people who *didn't* have to contend with something so rare, so public, so "handicapping." Did they lack—would I have lacked—connection with what they really wanted from life because they listened to too many voices, from people whose experience sounded similar to theirs? Did they move toward the middle, the safe place, rather than to the edge of their dreams, because that was what parents and loved ones and authority figures usually encouraged, well-meaning as they were?

Did you? Do you, still?

For me, *I had done the surviving part. Might as well try the thriving part.*

CHAPTER 6:

...But Also Find People to Trust Who Aren't You

It takes two to speak the truth—one to speak and another to hear.
—Henry David Thoreau

The person who affected how I felt about myself, more than any other, is Mary Ann.

Had I died in the days following the fire, I have no idea who would have been responsible for the insanely expensive medical care I got. Because I didn't die, my parents were on the hook for it, it appeared, because I was not eighteen when I entered the burning building. When I thought about it, and how my father was feeling about it, and what I looked like and what a difficult and long road to recovery it would be, I couldn't help but imagine him thinking: *I wish he would die. It would just be easier all around.*

But, like Harry Potter, I was the one who lived.

And there was a massive bill to pay.

We had a legal fight on our hands: the township's insurer's workers comp policy covered firefighters injured while serving on the job. But in this case, as I wrote earlier, the insurance company was balking at paying my medical costs since I was underage when I went into the building. Some of the newspaper accounts made it sound almost as if I had just been screwing around out there in the middle of the night. "Whether he took it on his own [to go inside] I don't know," the township solicitor was quoted in one story. In another, even the chief of my fire company was quoted in language I wouldn't exactly call supportive: "He [Brian] wanted to do a good job. He wanted to do what he had been trained to do" and "during the confusion and so forth he managed to get inside."

"Took it on his own"? "Managed"? Thanks, guys. Means a lot.

No way was that right, to punish my family further because I had followed what I was trained to do as a firefighter, because I had obeyed the orders of my superiors on the scene, and because it all happened before my eighteenth birthday. My dad called up a good friend, the best man at his wedding, a superior court judge and former attorney who recommended a law firm with an insurance and workers comp division. "They'll take care of this," he assured us.

For months we visited a partner at the firm's office, then he handed the case to another partner. The first time we visited the new attorney, I noticed his secretary. (That's what they called an administrative assistant, once upon a time.) Her name was Mary Ann Clark. She looked as Irish as could be, with an adorable smile. I was wearing my mask. I introduced myself to her, though all she was seeing of my face was eyes, the bottom of a nose, and a mouth.

I had to call the office frequently to ask questions or provide answers, and always found a way to extend the conversation. Soon, Mary Ann and I were talking about more than just the status and details of my case. I made her laugh. We got to know each other's voice and personality and soul first, before really spending time in person (aside from the rare office visit). I felt a need to talk about my future, maybe to demonstrate that I had plans, big plans, and wasn't defined by my past or fazed by this "setback." Our phone conversations started to exceed an hour. Finally, during one of our calls, I said, "Hey, you want to go to lunch?"

"I'm dating someone," she said. Unless I was kidding myself, she said it without much conviction. After all, by this point we were talking almost daily. I didn't realize that Mary Ann had already mentioned to her mother that the "funniest guy" would come to the office now and then, or call on the phone, and really make her laugh. And that she didn't know what this guy looked like because he always wore a mask.

Mary Ann turned me down.

On occasion, my father also had to talk to Mary Ann, for details about our lawsuit, and thought she was nice. The next time I mentioned lunch to Mary Ann, I had a better plan, almost foolproof. "Can I take you to lunch? If it makes it easier, my father can come along."

"I'm still dating someone," she reminded me. "If I'm going to lunch with you, I would have to break up with him."

"I'm not asking you to marry me," I said. "It's just lunch." *So Catholic*, I thought. "Break up with him! He's a loser."

"You don't even know him!"

She was right, of course. She never talked about him with me. I didn't know until later that his name was Chuck, that he grew up in Amish country, that he wasn't Amish himself, and that his big dream in life was to get a motorcycle. You can imagine the positive impression that last goal made on Mary Ann's parents.

"Listen, my Dad will be with me," I said to Mary Ann. "What's going to happen?"

This time she agreed. After a scheduled meeting with the attorney, my father and I took Mary Ann to lunch. My dad was his usual powerful, gruff, intimidating self. I hoped Mary Ann wouldn't be put off. She ate maybe three bites of salad.

A few days later, I asked Mary Ann to a Saturday night show—Rodney Dangerfield, Atlantic City. I was planning to go with my sister Renee and brother-in-law John, and I would get a fourth ticket. Again I was rebuffed. What I didn't know was that the night of the show, when Mary Ann was home doing nothing, she mentioned to her mother that I had asked her out again. Millie, who was no fan of Chuck's—she thought he was lazy and futureless—told her daughter, "These are the kinds of things you should be doing. Sitting here at home on a Saturday night is probably not the best thing for you."

Mary Ann was still dating Chuck when she agreed to go out with me on a date, just the two of us. It was a Friday night, days before I was heading down to Memphis to start the program in fire administration.

At the end of the date, she told me that she would tell Chuck she wanted to date other people, what sounded to me like a soft break-up. A week later, in Memphis, I received in the mail a Philadelphia Eagles t-shirt that Mary Ann had bought at a pre-season game that she had attended with her dad the previous weekend. It came with a handwritten note. I knew Chuck was history.

Ours was a long-distance relationship for months. I would see Mary Ann every four to six weeks, when I came back up to Philadelphia for a surgical procedure. Mary Ann's parents, Millie and Jim, were Irish Catholic and Democrats. Jim worked for the phone company, as had Millie before they started a family. When I first met them the following spring, I was wearing a full wig because I was losing my hair from alopecia, from the trauma of the fire. I had used Rogaine to make it grow, and the results were awful. The toupee wasn't much better. The Clarks hadn't been prepared for how bad my burns were. I'm not sure if it was because Mary Ann hadn't filled them in or if her parents simply had a hard time wrapping their minds around it. (They were not the first and—given the reaction I get to this day—I have yet to meet the last.) When I met Millie for the first time, she was in her garden, planting. I walked up and stood over her and said, "You must be Mrs. Clark. Nice to meet you." She could not have been more welcoming. She said it was a pleasure to meet me, she had heard a lot about me—and then she gave me a big hug. I walked into the house and for the first time met Mary Ann's dad Jim, her brother Bill—who also wrapped me in a huge hug—and her grandfather, who lived with them.

Sometimes Mary Ann would come down to Memphis to visit. I was glad Patty and Ray got to see me with her. They loved Mary Ann the moment they met her. This was all formative of my new version of myself: me in a relationship. I was still figuring out who this new

Brian Walsh was, and it was probably easier to comprehend if I could see myself from several angles, including who I was when I was with someone else. My life started feeling as if it had an engine to it, momentum, now that I had such a great partner in Mary Ann.

That fall, I entered the Clarks' kitchen, where Millie and Jim were sitting, and looked them each in the eye. "I'd like to ask your daughter to marry me," I said. "I love her very much and I promise I will always take care of her. You will never have to worry about that."

Where did all *that* come from? Who did I think I was? Maybe I added that last part out of desperation. Or expressed out loud my belief in myself, so it was on record. But why should they believe me?

"No," said Jim.

My brow wrinkled, as much as hardened skin grafts could wrinkle. "Really?" I said.

"Just kidding," he said.

Millie, who I knew genuinely liked me, put me through the wringer. *You're young, you're inexperienced, you're still getting your feet wet.* To be honest, I can't say the two of them looked overjoyed at any point during the conversation. Jim, my future father-in-law, had to be thinking, *Who is this young guy who wants to marry my daughter and has little professional experience?* Mary Ann's parents could see I was a hard worker, but I also didn't have obvious prospects.

Years later, Millie and Jim both claimed they believed my promise to them: that I would find a way, somehow, to make good on my word.

As much as self-confidence only works if it's truly you being confident in yourself, let's face it: we need evidence now and then that others out there believe in us, too. Or believe in us despite our not yet believing in ourselves. It can be our intelligence or personality, it can be our character—but there has to be something for them to admire, so we can, too. I was so fortunate that Mary Ann did that for me.

* * *

It would be nice to think that even if it's a really big problem you suffer from, at least it's only that one problem.

But it's never just one. Getting caught in a fire didn't give me some absence note in perpetuity excusing me from other significant hardships.

When I was younger, I suffered from terrible self-esteem because of my learning difficulties. Eventually I started to believe I was dumb. Then, when I was eighteen, I took a basic business course at Bucks County Community College. The first day the professor told us we were all required to subscribe to the *Wall Street Journal*. He made us read the "Heard on the Street" column, back when it was on the front page. In class we discussed that and related topics.

A few weeks into the course, the professor—Jack Smith was his name—asked me to remain after class. I wondered what I had done wrong. When the other students had left, he said, "I'd like you to stay with me for a bit. Ask you some questions."

"Okay," I said. What *could* I say?

"You participate very well in class," said Professor Smith, "but you test terribly."

"Yeah, it's always been that way," I said.

Professor Smith got on the classroom phone, and a few minutes later a woman entered the room. She asked me to read something, then write something, a couple of times. After a few minutes, she said, "Brian, you're dyslexic."

"What?" I said. I had no idea what that was.

"You see things differently from a lot of other people," she said. "You read some things backwards. Sometimes you write numbers backwards. It gets reversed in your head. It's not a cognitive thing. You're smart."

She worked with me, instilling strategies I use to this day—re-reading, slowing down, pronouncing the word. I needed to be very deliberate. If I read something very quickly, forget it. Even today, if I read too fast, I stop and tell myself, *Okay, you must have read that wrong. Go back.*

When I realized that dyslexia was something whose complications I could minimize with tools and tricks I could learn and master through persistence, it was a very liberating feeling. *Maybe I'm not the brightest bulb in the chandelier,* I thought, *but I'm competent.* I didn't take any special classes to help me. Just the time I spent with the teacher who diagnosed me. And being diligent.

Now and then, there have been moments of frustration caused by my learning problem. But armed with the knowledge to manage it, I never again got less than 90 on an exam, in Professor Smith's class or any other.

*   *   *

Without good-hearted people looking out for you, it becomes very difficult to achieve success—and I don't mean great wealth or a C-suite title or some other sign of prestige, but success at its most meaningful: success with people, in its many forms. For me, that success would have been unthinkable. I've been lucky to have some great role models, people who made it their business to guide me. And when I look back on it now, I realize that all of them were teaching me essentially the same lesson.

Example: My fire chief, Jack Quinn, always stressed to us that when we went to fight a fire, we had to keep in mind that *we were on people's property*. Saving lives came first, of course. But we should do everything in our power to respect and protect their homes, too. In other words: **Take respect to the next level.** Don't "surround and drown," as some companies did (and do), using so much water that it looks as if they want to flood the premises. Levittown No. 2 always tried first to ventilate a building by finding a window, not by chopping things open. We knew departments that just loved swinging the ax.

Another example: Tom Hartman, my boss at Hartman Financial Group, may not have been the greatest businessman, but was he ever a wonderful human being. I had just started at HFG when Mary Ann's first pregnancy turned complicated. At four months, she was put on bed rest. I was hesitant to mention it to Tom. I told myself I could soldier on, despite all my added responsibilities at home. But I soon saw how keeping it to myself could be irresponsible.

Tom was a big man, an ex-offensive lineman at Wake Forest, who smoked like a chimney and drove a big sled of a Mercedes. He and I had bonded from the start over our working-class backgrounds: his dad had been a heating and oil repairman. Tom always treated me well. He treated everyone well.

I finally worked up the nerve to tell him about Mary Ann's situation. A week later, she received in the mail a typewritten, beautifully expressed, *rhyming* letter from Tom. What boss does that? The note congratulated her on her pregnancy, sympathized over the difficulty she was going through, and promised that all her needs and mine would be taken care of. What business owner does that? He hired people to stop over at our home twice a week, for a few hours, to make our lives easier. Someone to clean, someone to prepare meals (for freezing), someone to do laundry and fold. For five months, Tom was unquestionably losing money on the Walshes.

And his gesture wasn't only about getting things taken care of or dealing with the logistics of a stressed employee and his bed-bound pregnant wife. Ultimately, it was about Mary Ann and me, as people. When I came out of the delivery room, ecstatic to tell my parents that Brian Jr. had been born, who was sitting there in the hospital waiting room with them? Tom.

Later, an even more profound role model for me was the esteemed Lester Rosen. The story goes that he died in his office, still working to help better the lives of his many clients, at age ninety-four. I don't know that he did, technically, but it's the way he lived that was so inspirational.

I met Lester twenty years ago, when he was already an icon in the insurance industry. As a young man at Wharton, he was a student of the renowned Solomon Huebner, founder of what became the American College of Financial Services, and both of them were leading advocates of education in the financial services industry. Then Lester set out on his own in the life insurance business. He eventually devised and espoused what he dubbed the "Whole Person" concept. Whole Person meant a type of approach and success that could not be defined by your career alone. It had to be about other things, too—what you were giving back to society, what you did with your family, how you treated your fellow human beings, how you lived your life and took care of your health. He liked to say that in his conversations with his clients, he "talked life before talking life insurance." Lester first proposed this "radical" Whole Person notion in the 1950s. It resonated with people then; today it's an accepted premise in the industry and beyond. Lester lived his own life the Whole Person way.

I had the pleasure and honor of meeting him at a few financial conferences. He was exactly as advertised. He took genuine interest in everyone, not just with the perfunctory "How's business? Good, good—so anyway…" that's so standard among phonies.

When I ran into Lester once in London, he remembered my name. I'm sure he knew thousands of people. (True, probably few of them looked like me.) He was by then in his eighties. Yet without prompting from anyone, he asked me, "Brian, how are things in Philadelphia? What's going on? Can we have lunch with you and Mary Ann?" I can't tell you what an impression that made on me. It was like a magic trick, except there was no trickery. It was the result of living a life well and thoughtfully, full of only the things that matter.

Of course Lester followed through. Over lunch with his wife Pat, Mary Ann, and me, Lester exuded nothing but real caring. Again, it was not just "How's your career going?" but much more basic stuff, like, "What are you struggling with?" and "What can I help you with?" At one point he asked, "What are you doing with your free time?"

"You call it free time, Lester," I joked. "I call it no time." By then I was still volunteering with the fire service, coaching the kids' Little League teams, and wondering how I could do everything. "Lester, the Whole Person concept is great, but you've got to have time to sleep."

I got to see him two or three times a year. He wasn't the kind of mentor who called you once a week, but he was a great role model. He was from Memphis, so we shared that bond, too.

He had the same assistant until he died. It was something like a sixty-year working relationship. She didn't retire either. A few months before Lester passed away, the story goes, he had to give up his practice because he was legally blind. He couldn't take the mandatory Continuing Education classes online, which forced him to give up his license. But he kept employing his assistant so she would read his mail each day and he could sign his name where needed. He still made calls to clients.

Lester lived what he preached. He enjoyed a long, good, productive, generous life, and worked until the day he died, maybe literally. Hard to beat that as your story.

* * *

You never know who is going to turn into a mentor, for which aspect of your life. Did I know that a burn unit nurse named Jim would be so instrumental to my story, such a model of compassion and skill, that Mary Ann and I would one day make him godfather to our firstborn?

Among the most important influences on my parenting were Patty and Ray, watching how they dealt with the dozens of things that came up daily with their sons, years before I was even thinking about having a family, but what I saw stuck. I witnessed how they didn't let issues that were annoying but ultimately unimportant take on more weight than they should. I saw what they let the boys do and not do. I watched the way they did things in their everyday lives and I made little mental checkmarks. *That's a good thing. That's another good thing.* Sometimes I even tagged along to PTA meetings at Chris's school. If you can swing it, it's useful for your future as a parent to hang around someone else's family home as a twenty-year-old, to see how it's done, bad or good. Growing up in your own home, especially as the youngest, you can't really appreciate what goes into it, not from that angle. There's no question that Patty and Ray helped me raise my family because of what I learned from them. I think they even helped me be a better businessman, too. Taking to the role of oldest of the "kids" in the family made me more comfortable with being in charge, helped me know what that felt like. Years later, when I started my own firm, I was confident that I had the leadership makeup to do it.

* * *

What was that one, consistent lesson I learned from great role models like Jack Quinn, Tom Hartman, Lester Rosen, and Patty and Ray?

There are right ways to do things and wrong ways. ***Believe it or not, for all the variety and choice in the world, there's always an absolutely right way to do things.***

The right way does not always mean going by the book. In fact, it probably *rarely* means that. (Think about it: why are big companies so much less appealing to work for? Everything is by the book—or claims to be.) If a couple guys on the Levittown volunteer fire force had not followed their own compassionate, ethical, brave instincts and instead had listened to those running the show, I would have died that night in the Edgely Run Apartment complex, Building A, third floor. But Johnny Glasson and Kenny Sims weighed the factors quickly. Or maybe they rushed in because they *didn't* weigh the factors; screw the factors! They knew all the good and bad reasons to go back in or not go back in, considered their training and experience…and they went back in to rescue a fallen comrade. So much for the book.

And the episode with Tom Hartman taught me almost the same lesson. For one, whether he himself arranged the help we got in taking care of our home or he relied on someone very competent to do it, there was never a glitch—or maybe there was, but it was taken care of so quickly and completely, neither Mary Ann nor I ever noticed. The crucial takeaway for me: ***When you do a favor for someone, however big or small, do it all the way—not halfway or three-quarters of the way. Do it in such a way that all they have to do is sit back and enjoy and appreciate the gesture.*** So many times, I'll see people make a half-stab at a nice gesture—drive you most of the way to your destination but not door-to-door; pick up the tab for a meal but skimp on the tip—and while I suppose it's nicer than no gesture at all, it also says, "You mean this much to me—but not *that* much." Instead, it should just be the first six words of that statement. That's it. I learned that from Tom. The way I try to treat people at my company is inspired partly by his example. When my assistant Amy's father passed away suddenly, we told her to use the company credit card for whatever she needed—flying out to California, buying flowers, having meals delivered while the family was grieving, anything. I told her to take her time, that we would all be fine for the time being (as vital as she is to me and the firm), that I didn't want her calling in to check on work. I didn't want to go halfway—you know, *Take all the time you need but please check your email at least twice a day.* Tom's influence.

And Lester's ultimate message? There's a right way to live a life and a bunch of ways that aren't quite right. The Whole Person way reminds you that career success is just one of many metrics. Without awareness of the other areas of importance, especially those focused on other people (how you spend time with your family and friends, what you do for those in need)—well, that's not the right way.

* * *

You never know when and where your life guides are going to appear, the good ones (Watch what he or she does!) and the bad (Do the opposite of what he or she does!). You can try to seek them out. You can get recommendations from people you trust. But that's not how you usually find them. I think they find you as much as you find them. I keep my eyes and heart open at all times so I don't miss the next opportunity. Because I know I can't do it on my own. I know there are people out there who have been where I have, one way or another; I know they got to an even better place, a place I'd like to get to.

If you look open to it, your mentor will know you when he or she sees you.

CHAPTER 7:

Throw the First Punch[*]

You grow up the day you have the first real laugh at yourself.
—Ethel Barrymore

Whether I grew into the person I was always destined to be or some hybrid of Before Fire Brian Walsh and After Fire Brian Walsh, I knew this: I could not be embarrassed. I wouldn't be. Even when I should have been, I wasn't. I'm completely bald now, but when I started to lose my hair, a development that makes many men self-conscious, I started taking Rogaine. My hair began growing back because the loss was caused by a certain type of alopecia. It wasn't coming in fast enough for my taste, though, so I thought, *Screw this*, and shaved it and bought a toupee (the cost covered, by the way, by workers comp). I guess you could say that many toupee- and wig-wearers are engaged in a form of mask-wearing, hiding behind something in plain sight. So I guess back then I still *could* be embarrassed.

And then, before you knew it, I couldn't be. I don't know the exact moment it happened, but the toupee stopped being a mask and instead

---

* May not apply to all readers.

became a prop. I would be out at a bar with friends or sitting in the passenger seat of a car at a red light. If I noticed people looking at me too long, which was always, I was sure I knew what they were thinking: *What the hell happened to HIM?*

And I realized, *Wait, I have a great prop! On my head!* I would grab the back of my toupee and pull it down toward my neck. Then I would push it forward until it hung over my eyes. The same people who couldn't look away? Now they *really* couldn't look away. As a final flourish, I would lift the toupee from my head, almost as if it were taking a bow, and put it back on.

* * *

In the fall of 2017 I was out in Los Angeles visiting my son Matt, and we decided to see a movie. I let him pick because I didn't care; I'm always happy just to be with my kids, and I see Matt least of the three since he's in California. The theater lights dimmed, we sat through a few trailers, credits rolled for the feature, and in the opening scene a bear runs through the woods.

On fire.

I leaned over to Matt. "You're kidding me, right?" I whispered.

"What?" he said.

"You brought me to *this* movie?"

"Oh, you're over it. Stop."

We watched *Only the Brave,* based on the true story of the Granite Mountain Hotshots, starring Josh Brolin, about the Yarnell Hill Fire in Arizona in 2013, one of the deadliest wildfires in U.S. history. I enjoyed it, don't get me wrong. It was well done. But afterward, as we were leaving the theater, I said to Matt, "You brought me to a movie about nineteen firemen dying in a forest fire."

He looked at me. "You're *over* it," he repeated.

He was right. I was over it by then, more than thirty-five years after the event. Still, there were parts of the movie that disturbed me (and could disturb those who had never fought a fire, too). *I* wouldn't have picked it for the evening's entertainment.

But Matt's movie choice, if a little dark, highlighted a quality in our family dynamic, and my own: When we approach my "situation," we don't ignore it. We confront it. Occasionally unpack it. Very often joke about it.

* * *

Disney's Hollywood Studios theme park, near Orlando, years ago. The kids are approximately thirteen, ten, and eight years old. We're waiting to get on the Rock 'n' Roller Coaster Starring Aerosmith, standing in one of those snaking lines that keeps doubling back on itself. A pack of teens a couple of years older than Brian Jr., a few snake segments behind us, is looking our way and talking under their breath. I catch only bits of what they're saying but it's enough: *the guy's face.* Katie, standing in front of me and not looking in their direction, now turns toward them, having obviously heard, too. Maybe she has made out more of the conversation than I have. Immediately I grip her shoulders and forcefully turn her back around, facing me and away from them.

"You can't worry about what people think," I tell her in the kindest, least pained voice I can manage. "If it doesn't matter to me, it shouldn't matter to you."

Hilton Head, a couple years later. Brian Jr., Matt, and I are in the men's locker room following two sets of tennis. I stand at the urinal, and a man in tennis whites enters and takes his place a couple urinals over. He turns to me, studying me in profile for a moment—not something a guy typically does to another guy in the bathroom.

"Wow, you make Viktor Yushchenko look good," he says.

"Excuse me?" I say, slightly flustered, which doesn't usually happen.

He smiles nervously, zips up fast, and disappears.

I have to move quickly to stop Brian Jr. from chasing the guy outside and kicking his ass. Viktor Yushchenko, at that time, was president of Ukraine. His face was severely pockmarked and jaundiced, likely from dioxin poisoning by a political rival. If an American knew about him from the news, that's what he'd know: the severe facial disfigurement.

I really should have said something to the tennis-playing asshole. But such open rudeness and unkindness are pretty rare. Why would people with those thoughts think it's wise to vocalize them to me? If they happen to glance at me, and the glance lingers, or they can't help but return to my face after a few seconds of forcing themselves to look away…I can't fault people for that. I won't. But such plain, unadulterated meanness isn't something I experience often. When it happens, I try not to let it bother me. I can't, if I don't want it to bother my kids. I know each of them would fight for me with everything they have. I simply won't let my appearance bother me, or bother me anymore, at least outwardly. In trying to be strong enough to live that idea consistently, I believe I helped make my children even more substantial individuals than they were already becoming.

Still, I live in the world. Not everyone has to devise a strategy for how to be in the world, especially if you find yourself "normal," part of the crowd, whatever that means. Sometimes it means being male or white or straight or able-bodied. Having a normal, smooth face. You're just in the world, and often you don't even notice it, and your first impulses are usually fine, because the world seems to have been made with you in mind. Having a badly disfigured face is certainly not one of the norms, and made me feel for others who feel marginalized in a way I had not before. After the accident, I had to find a way to be in the world so that everything was not this big decision, so that I could just *be* in a way that felt natural to me. My solution, it turned out, was to be as open and straightforward as possible about myself, my physical self, my face. How could I be a straight-shooter and a self-believer and a good salesman and a good soul, but also act as if there was nothing unusual about me? That would be hypocritical. Or it would make me look blind to myself, lacking in self-awareness. Pretending has a limit. So I had to devise a way to anticipate the long looks. A way to handle or defuse insensitive or ignorant comments. A way to turn something that could be awkward and hard to get past into a non-issue, or (maybe this was asking way too much) even something positive. A way to win over wary strangers.

My solution? Always throw the first punch.

Not literally. I try to disarm people with self-deprecating jokes. Was this something I learned *because* of my accident? I don't know. I was a wisecracking teenager, as the mean and awful Sister Saint Angela would have confirmed. Regardless of where the impulse was born, I needed to be funny, even outrageous, to address the total unfunniness of my situation. Once, at a company banquet, the manager of the venue was looking for my brother Ed, an executive VP at my firm at the time, to settle the bill. The manager was mistakenly directed to me instead.

"You can give the bill to my brother," I told the manager.

"What does he look like?" he asked, scanning the room.

"Like me," I said to the poor guy, "only not burned."

If I find myself in a hotel lobby or a lodge or someone's home and I'm seated next to a fireplace, I might borrow from my nephew Danny, back when he was a four-year-old saying the most honest thing that came into his head, and refer to myself as "Mr. Burnie."

When preparing to deliver a speech at a recent conference, they asked me what song I wanted as exit music. I said the Talking Heads' "Burning Down the House." Inappropriate? They played it, but I'm not sure many people got the joke.

Or I'll open a box of newly delivered pizza and say, "Look, a mirror!"

Okay, that one's harsh. Sometimes the response is crickets or pained smiles. What makes it harsh, though? Yes, it makes people uncomfortable to think I think I look that bad. But I'm doing it to ease *their* discomfort. It's a fine line deciding how much is too much, deciding if my idea of funny is yours.

Once, my business colleague Jeff Silverman and I were invited to dine with a corporation's board member and another one of their executives amid a very charged and uncertain time for the company. The dinner conversation was fine but perfunctory; you could feel the tension from the two of them. The dessert came: the makings for baked Alaska. When the waiter approached our table and set the concoction aflame right next to me, I looked up at him. In my driest delivery, I uttered maybe my single most favorite word: "Really?" I couldn't stop right there. "I can't just have regular Alaska? Can't you bake it just long enough to pull it out so it lives?"

The waiter looked miserable. I placed my hand on his arm gently and smiled, letting him know I was kidding.

Yet the moment lightened the mood, as I suspected it might. The four of us at the table sat for another two hours, joking and laughing. My self-effacing comment helped change the atmosphere from a standard business meeting to a night where people leave as friends. Was it easy for me, inside, to make such a crack? Actually, it was. I mean, look at me: I've looked like this for decades. I live a good life. It's a life I've lived with this face. Could there be a connection? Maybe, with all the twists and turns that any life offers, I would have had a much less rich time of it without this "special" circumstance. If I had looked "normal."

So how can I not like this face?

By joking as I do, especially when it's pretty aggressive, I take control of my situation by almost cornering the other person into responding to my *joke* about me, not to the actual me. Some people could say it's an obvious defense mechanism, and I won't disagree. ***In a life full of things we can't control, which parts can we really own?*** I don't know how conscious or subconscious my responses are in these potentially awkward moments, but I know I won't leave it to others to own them. I'm the one who has experience defusing it. Except for the occasional a-hole sidling up to me at a tennis club urinal, it's extremely rare for someone who has laid eyes on me for the first time to feel bold enough to bring up the subject without me doing so first. That's why kids are so refreshing. They can't be bothered with protocol or hiding what they're feeling, and their questions are rooted in curiosity, not malice.

Not many people have such jarring facts about themselves, right there for everyone to see, as I do. But everyone's got something about which they're self-conscious. Height, weight, hair, clothes, something. If it makes you feel insecure, would a light-hearted comment about it help? Help *you*? By giving expression to what you feel others may feel but don't want to say? Yes, you have to be comfortable doing it. And there's a fine line between coming off as modest and self-aware and charming, on one hand, and self-hating, on the other. But the ability to take control of what feels like a disadvantage and to neutralize it: that can be very liberating. (As I indicated by the asterisk in the chapter title, this is probably not for everyone.)

Maybe my joking is perverse. It's seeking an advantage when I feel disadvantaged by my appearance. But I know that once I break through that barrier and disarm people, they have an extra incentive to like me, root for me, even want to work with me.

* * *

It's my personality to throw the first punch. I get that such aggressiveness is not for everyone. But I do it to make this clear: do not for one second feel sorry for me. You can feel a lot of things for me—but not pity. *Oh, the Burn Guy.* Once, as I was boarding a plane in Calgary, a legless man in a wheelchair, who had been escorted down the jet bridge to the plane entrance, lifted himself out of the chair and walked on his arms onto the plane, down the aisle, and flipped himself right into his seat. As I and everyone behind me watched, I remember thinking: *Do not feel bad for him.* **Admire** *him.*

I don't want to be treated any differently from anyone else. To the friends and family who knew me my first seventeen and a half years and saw how I changed and how I stayed the same, I was not "the guy who got burned." And I refused to be that for people who met me after the fire. If they did see me that way, if they simply couldn't get that out of their head and always considered it one of the top "facts" about me, then I needed to figure out how to change that perception. I never wanted to meet you as Burn Guy. I wanted to meet you as Brian, with all of Brian's strengths and weaknesses, feelings and thoughts. I am *not* foremost a victim. I'm not a victim at all, in fact. Like I said: look at my life. How am I a victim?

So while I don't look at myself as the burned guy, at some point I'll probably make a joke about being the burned guy. There's a difference.

I also believe that throwing the first punch is an act of generosity, not brash obnoxiousness. By throwing the first punch, I feel I'm making it easy on others. *Look: if he jokes about it himself, then it's fair game.*

There's one more major advantage to this whole strategy of mine: more opportunities for laughter and good storytelling. Many years ago, Phil Ring, a potential new client I enjoyed immediate chemistry with over the phone—we were joking and even insulting each other five minutes into our first-ever conversation—wondered if I could drop off some documents at his home. We had yet to meet in person. It happened to be Halloween. "I won't be there," said Phil, "but my very young daughter and the babysitter will. So just don't wear your Freddy Krueger mask." I said nothing. I dropped the papers off at Phil's without incident, knowing he and I would meet in person for the first time a few days later when he would stop by my office with the countersigned documents. He was sitting in my waiting room when I walked out. When he first laid eyes on me, I couldn't help myself.

"Freddy Krueger here," I said. He looked stricken.

Phil has been one of my best friends for decades now.

The gift that comes with surviving tragedy is a greater understanding of your fellow human. Greater empathy. I wish tragedy on no one, but if, God forbid, it should visit you, you no longer ever put yourself above others (if you ever did). Other people suddenly *are* you. Strangers are you.

I cannot be embarrassed. **I have no fear of new situations because I'm not afraid of what people might think of me.** I'm not saying I'm not bothered if people don't like me. But I won't let it stop me from doing what I think I should. People see the "worst" of me the moment they lay eyes on me. So why not just be who I am, which is so much better than what they may think I am? Nothing holds me back. I'll say what I want.

*   *   *

I can use my face as a laugh line, but if there's something I don't want to do, I can also use it as a way to cut things off. I don't like to go down that road, but every now and then, I have to. I did so several years ago to get out of one of the "obligations" I dislike most in business: corporate retreats. I don't do well on them. You sit for three days holding hands while singing songs of kinship and doing trust exercises. I don't need a trip into the woods to figure out if the people I work with are trustworthy. I had better know that already.

I was working for Mass Mutual at the time, in an office building on Philadelphia's Rittenhouse Square, and my boss wanted to take the whole management team (about twenty of us) to Pecos River, New Mexico, for a team-building retreat. Now, my current business partner and I have taken our own company go-kart racing and done occasional camaraderie stuff like ballgames and renting out a room at a nice restaurant. But "trust exercises"? Yeah, that's not happening.

My Mass Mutual superior, Tim, must have had his reasons for the Pecos River trip. But I stepped into his office to inform him I was not going.

"What do you mean you're not going?" he said.

"I'm not going," I said.

"It's not a choice."

"Yeah, it is."

"No, it's not."

"You're mandating that as part of my employment with you?"

Tim paused. "No," he admitted.

"Then it's a choice. And my choice is, I'm not going."

The upshot of our exchange soon circulated around the office. It hurt a few of my colleagues that I wasn't planning to join them. When the CFO heard about it, he confided to me that he didn't want to go either, but he felt trapped. "Man, I just can't do that," he told me.

"I did," I said.

"I know!" he said, shaking his head. "Tim told me himself."

They worried that if I stuck to my guns, then others who hated corporate retreats would also bow out. Tim approached me again and tried one last tack. "If you don't go," he said, "then how are you going to prove to your fellow management team that you're a courageous individual?"

He was lucky I didn't hit him.

"Tell you what, Tim," I said, after taking a deep breath. "You have each of the members of the management team walk around Rittenhouse Square just once, at lunchtime, with the mask I wore for two years, and when they all come back in here after that courageous feat, I'll go to Pecos River."

I never went to Pecos River.

*   *   *

One problem with a personal calamity this big is that people can't help but divide your life in two. Before the Fire, After the Fire.

To be honest, maybe the person who experiences the calamity does that himself, too, because it's sometimes hard to remember which traits you always had and which ones were survival reactions to what happened. For example: Would my professional successes—and failures—have happened without the fire? I'm sure **there's an urgency to how I work and live that surpasses what I was naturally wired for.** I was a happy-go-lucky boy throughout Catholic grade school, not the rebel I was sometimes made out to be. I was a joker. I would say something funny or absurd in a straight-faced way, until the other person would say, "Wait—are you serious?" I'd say, "No, I'm not." So I pushed it, to be funny or different—but only up to a point. I was fine with a certain amount of discomfort and absurdity, but I wasn't a misfit. I had a taste for adventure. I loved cars. My first one, a 1962 Buick Special, I bought for two hundred bucks, and the only place you could get parts for it was a scrapyard. I liked driving on the fast side—but I also had a sense of responsibility. Was one of these qualities more likely to rise or fall as I got older? The combination of traits I have now—would they be different if I had never been burned? Did I develop a whole new set of traits I never had?

Whatever the answer, after the accident I knew that I needed either to hold on to whatever optimism I already had in me or develop a new batch real quick. Over the years, I have seen and heard of so many people who went through terrible ordeals—being burned, getting cancer or other debilitating and potentially fatal diseases, suffering the loss of family members, especially children—and one of the obvious and most common reactions is hopelessness and surrender. Bitterness, a turn to drugs or alcohol, anything that numbs. It's understandable. It's impossible to fault people in such scenarios for some "weakness" of character.

But my very close friend Joe, a doctor, has told me about many cancer patients he has dealt with, and while of course none of them wanted cancer, so many have said that in numerous ways it was a rare gift. They had been coasting through life. They needed to hit bottom. ***We know intellectually that hitting bottom is often what we need, but it's very hard to do it "on your own" if you don't have to.*** Once they *had* to, though? They got the blessing of a new perspective on their life, their relationships, their spouses or partners, their families, their careers, their tendencies, the way they spent their waking hours. In almost every case they told themselves, *If I make it through this ordeal, I am going to re-examine my priorities.* They grabbed their misfortune and used it to propel themselves forward. The cancer or other terrible circumstance got them to refine or redefine who they were. Once they got through their ordeal, they had a "Bring it on!" mentality. *I made it through that, so what **can't** I do?* There's leverage to experiencing tragedy and coming out the other side.

I was not—I am not—immune to dark thoughts. There are times I have been deeply disappointed in my fellow man. (I once had t-shirts printed up for myself and several friends that read, "PEOPLE…NOT A BIG FAN.") I have questioned the existence of a higher power. One night early in my ordeal at the burn center, I thought that I was on the verge of death. I remember thinking, *This is the end. I'm gone. It's over.* It was so hard to comprehend yet I knew it. Things could easily have gone either way, which meant that could easily have been my last night.

When I woke and it was the next day, I didn't know whom I was supposed to thank or praise for not dying, God or Jesus Christ or Buddha or the Dalai Lama or the overnight nurse. But I was so grateful I was still alive—terrified and in horrible pain and in shock and very, very grateful. Finding myself unexpectedly, gratefully alive, I told myself: I am not ready to go. I will fight death to the death.

But *I wasn't yet fighting for life. Just fighting off death. They're not the same thing.*

Just because you don't want to die doesn't mean you're "home free." If that's your frame of mind—*just don't die*—there's still a real danger of becoming a recluse. My doctor friend said that was not uncommon.

There was no great, inspiring Knute Rockne moment that helped me make the pivot from not wanting to die to wanting to live the best life I could. I just knew instinctively that having a certain amount of laughter would make it easier to get to that future place and make the present more enjoyable, too.

CHAPTER 8:

Listen, That's All

When people show you who they are, believe them the first time.
—Maya Angelou

The stench of burnt human flesh is truly horrendous. Even if you
didn't know it, you know it. If you have actually smelled that smell,
you think you won't ever forget it.

The first time I was back at St. Agnes, when I was nineteen years old,
the smell practically knocked me over. I had returned because a nurse
there had contacted me. They had just received a patient, twenty years
old, burned worse than I had been.

Glen was from Wilkes-Barre, near Scranton. His car had been rear-
ended and blew up. His parents asked the nurses if there was anyone who
had been through something similar and could come talk to them, so the
nurse called me. It was my first time back since I had been discharged
more than a year earlier. It wasn't an official visit initiated by the hospital
social workers. Considering how careful they were about outsiders entering the burn ICU, I was told to show up after eight o'clock one night and
the nurse would sneak me in.

That's when the smell nearly knocked me off my feet. I went in to visit Glen, so young, and I thought, *Oh, god.* All the tubes in him. I felt as if I was looking at myself, except Glen was in far worse shape. His face, everything. An awful picture.

I talked to him for a few minutes. With all the tubes he couldn't respond. But his eyes followed me.

"You're gonna get better," I told him. I didn't know I would be lying to this stranger until the words came out. Here it was, my first time back, and I realized I had to tell Glen that things were not as bad as they seemed. I had been told that Glen was burned over 95 percent of his body. You didn't have to do the sobering math to know there was zero chance he was going to survive this. "You're gonna get through this," I told him.

I didn't know how much of what I said was registering, but from his eye movements it was clear that something was getting through. At one point he reached for my hand.

Afterward, I spoke with his parents in the waiting room.

"Thank you very much for coming and talking to my son," Glen's dad said.

"He's going to fight really hard," I told them, with no basis whatsoever.

"Is he going to look like you?" asked the mom.

"I hope so," I said, thinking it was the answer she would want to hear.

"Oh, God," she said.

I caught the nurse's eyes. She winced. Glen's mother, I realized, had interpreted my answer exactly opposite from how I meant it. She thought: *How terrible, if my son ends up looking like you.* I thought: *How great, if he looks like me, because that would mean he survived.* How *lucky* to look like me after it was all over.

It brought another realization, a more important one: I wasn't hurt by Glen's mom's reaction. I didn't feel bad for myself, only gut-wrenchingly terrible for her and her husband, and of course Glen. I totally understood her response. A year and a half earlier, I had been where her son was, though ultimately with a different prognosis for survival. Once upon a time I had heard doctors talking, sometimes in hushed tones, about skin grafts and what they could "do for Brian." I hadn't known anyone who had gone through an experience like mine, ghastly burns all over the face, so I was free to start telling (lying to) myself, *I'll have the skin grafts, and over time I'll look just like I did.* That's how I came to show Dr. White, the plastic surgeon in Memphis, my high school yearbook photo. Talk about the optimism of youth. Talk about deluded.

I was positive that at that moment, that's what Glen's mom was thinking about her boy: *It looks really bad—really, really bad—but this is fixable. Somehow.* It was extremely likely that she, too, had no experience with severe burns, so this was where she landed. She was not being mean to me. It was a valid human reflex. Self-preservation. A mother's wish. Her reality in that moment was simply: *Oh, they didn't quite get it right with you, sad young man. But they will with my Glen.*

Afterward, when the nurse who had called me to pay the visit walked me out, she said, "Oh my God, Brian, I'm so sorry."

"What are you sorry for? I would have said the same thing, in her shoes. If I didn't say it, I would have thought it. When I was here the first time, I said the same thing to myself."

I was scheduled to see Glen the following week, but I got a call the morning of my visit that he had died the previous night.

* * *

Sometimes life is really hard to figure out, and people do things that leave you with no choice but to scratch your head. A lot of the time, though, maybe more than we think, life is fairly straightforward. Most people are usually pretty easy to understand.

Claude, a seventy-year-old man who became a quadriplegic four years earlier when his car was rear-ended by a tractor-trailer, was searching for someone to manage his finances. He had met with a number of financial advisors before me, looking for the right fit. I'm sure they all told him about their expected annualized returns.

When I met him, after we exchanged hellos, I asked, "What do you want to have happen here?"

"You're the first person to ask me that," he said.

We discussed his goals and dreams. He wanted to buy a home for each of his kids. Some smaller stuff, too, but that was the main thing.

It's possible that Claude recognized in me a comrade, someone who had also suffered great physical damage firsthand, and carried it around with him every day. Maybe he thought I had a more highly developed understanding of what his life was like and how it feels to have had it monumentally and forever changed in an instant.

And yet, I honestly don't think that was it. Had one of the other financial managers that Claude met before me, some conventional-looking man or woman with no obvious physical handicap, *really listened* to Claude, they would have won the account. What do I mean by "really listened?" **When people get talking, listen to where they end up, relatively quickly. Talk less; they always do the work for you.** A couple of years ago, when Brian Jr. had just started at our firm, Richard, a gentleman in his seventies and one of my long-time clients, came by the office. Practically before I was even finished asking how he was doing, he had his wallet out to show me a photograph of his twin toddler grandsons. We talked for two hours. My door was open and Brian passed by the office a few times during the conversation.

After Richard left, Brian came by my office. "Why didn't you ask him what he wants you to do for him?" he asked.

"He told me," I said.

"You spent maybe three minutes on business. The rest of the conversation all you guys did was talk family, travel, retirement, golf, and the Eagles."

"Brian, that wasn't the 'rest' of the conversation. *That was the conversation!* The reason the retired are retired and the travelers are traveling is because I help them get there. If they want to sit there and talk about the trips they've taken, I'm going to sit and listen to it. And I'm going to be interested in it. Because when I look back at my original notes from when I first met them, those were their goals. They wanted to travel and retire. You know what I picked up from this conversation? He told me he was expecting another grandchild. So he's basically telling me, 'Should I do anything special to prepare for that?' He's telling me, 'Could you give my son a call and talk to him about his financial planning?' He's saying, 'When they start looking for a bigger house, how do they set themselves up for that?'"

Richard told me everything I needed to know about his financial concerns and hopes, just not in those words. The numbers part of our relationship would take care of itself on our computer screens.

If you listen to what people are saying, and if there's real emotion and engagement in your half of the conversation, they'll tell you everything. And they'll want you to be the one to listen to them next time around, and the time after that.

Take people at face value. That sounds a little clever coming from me. But I've come to see that I can approach almost anyone and find common ground, so long as I really listen and I'm really there. All people want to do is connect. Bottom line.

*　*　*

We all have a need to share, even if we don't admit it right away. And we usually want to share with people we trust to understand our unique experience.

When I was much younger—at nineteen, twenty, twenty-one years of age—I loved hanging out with my friends at a local Chi-Chi's, just sitting at the bar drinking. One night, three of us were hanging out— Mike Smith, Tod Milburn, and me—and we started chatting with two women, one in her twenties, the other in her late thirties (guessing). The older woman immediately focused on me, genuinely entranced by my face. She squeezed in to be near me, which was a nice change: women didn't often just approach me—or if they did, they seemed at pains to pretend that nothing was different or wrong with me.

"Were you burned?" she asked. She seemed genuine, not as if she was just making conversation. Still, I couldn't help my knee-jerk sarcasm. And I was a couple margaritas in.

"What gave you the first clue?" I asked.

Before long, the woman invited me out to the parking lot to show me something in her car.

I wasn't gone long, but when I walked back into Chi-Chi's, Mike said, "Where did you go? What the hell's going on?" He seemed almost angry that I had disappeared.

"She told me a story about herself," I said.

"What? What does that mean?"

"Eight years ago, she's making spaghetti. She's carrying the pot of boiling water to the sink, she slips, the water spills on her chest and she burns her breasts."

He was quiet for a moment, taking it in. "Are you kidding me?" he said.

"No," I said calmly. "She took me to her car to show me her burned tits."

* * *

A few years ago, I was invited to talk about customer service to a big insurance company in Nebraska. Their call center had developed bad work habits and poor morale and I was asked to come address their people.

"Look," I told the sixty or so women and men seated before me, "you all answer an eight hundred number, yet you don't know the person on the other end of the phone. But in a way you already know the most important thing: *This person called.* And this is a life insurance company. The person called you at one of the most desperate times in their life. They just lost a spouse, a parent. Somebody in their family just died. They're probably asking you for a beneficiary form. You're trained to get their address and mail it out to them. Do you understand how important you are to them, right then? Somebody provided them with this life insurance policy. It might have been fifty or sixty or seventy years ago. It might have been a year ago. At the moment the policy was purchased, this company made a promise to the person who took out that policy that when they died, their family was going to get this money to help them through that very, very tough time years down the road and beyond. Well, we're down that road with them. Right now. The dreaded event has occurred, and the beneficiary is on the phone with you, making sure that promise is kept. Your job is absolutely crucial to keeping the promise to the person on the other end of the phone. Understand that. Understand the impact you have on that."

I noticed an older woman a few rows back, sobbing. *Why is she crying?* I wondered. I thought maybe she felt I was there to berate her and her colleagues, get them to step it up. Not quite as vicious as Alec Baldwin's character in *Glengarry Glen Ross*, but there to shake them awake. Always Be Compassionate.

I asked if anyone had questions.

The sobbing woman was the first arm up. "I don't have a question," she said. "I just want to say something. I've worked here for seventeen years and no one has ever told me that. And I really feel important now."

I could have said, "There's the problem, right there. You should have known that all these years." How do we go so long not letting people who do such hard work, who simply want to feel valued for their work, not know something as basic and true as that?

Instead, I simply said to her, "You *are* important."

For everyone who comes through your door at work: make them feel happy by appreciating their effort. ***Everyone wants to be appreciated for the work they spend so many hours of their lives doing.***

If possible, learn the names of their spouse or partner or children or dog. If you're not naturally a good listener—and you may not be, and you surely have other talents—then at least try to teach yourself to remember names. That goes a long way to convincing people that they matter.

CHAPTER 9:

Be Yourself, Don't Sell Yourself

A man cannot be comfortable without his own approval.
—Mark Twain

You trust firefighters because they risk their lives *for strangers*. You trust parents because, well, because you do. Why would you ever trust a financial advisor?

Once I had purged myself of the need to be a firefighter, I had to find something else to do with my life. To be honest, I never stopped to consider that what I ended up choosing—providing people with a sense of financial security and protecting them from loss, among other things—was really just another version of what I used to do. Once I wanted to save lives. Now, I help save futures.

I have been fortunate to enjoy some success in my field, and I assure you I am no genius, not even close. I am not extraordinary in so many ways. I took my first accounting course at Saint Joseph's University. After my second night class, the professor pulled me aside and said, "Brian, don't waste your money here. If you're planning on staying in business, go down the street." I did, to the American College of Financial Services, the country's lone accredited college for financial services.

There were times I knew how close I was to being in over my head. When I was just twenty-two, my Mutual of Omaha boss, Joe Marino, who still commuted from Long Island, would leave the Bensalem office on Thursday afternoon and not return until Tuesday morning, leaving me in charge of a bunch of fifty-year-olds. It was a nice vote of confidence, but I had passed my certification exam not even a year earlier.

And about my learning problem: Reading was my biggest challenge, inverting letters. (Writing was never a problem.) Occasionally I inverted numbers, too. How does a financial advisor handle *that*? At a staff meeting some years ago, I unknowingly inverted a number on the whiteboard, sat down, and we all continued talking until one of my staff said, "The seven is backward."

I looked at the whiteboard. "Jesus!" I tried to laugh it off.

The staffer said, "For a second, I thought you were dyslexic."

I smiled. "I am." *What the hell*, I thought. I had never said it publicly.

"No way," she said.

"Yep," I said—not as if some weight had been lifted from my shoulders, but more matter-of-fact. More like, *This clearly hasn't ruined my life so I might as well be upfront about it.* The numbers 7 and 4 gave me particular trouble.

"Ooh," she said, trying to make light or sense of it. To this day I think a part of her thinks I had to be kidding.

* * *

In my business, what we sell is intangible. We're really only as good as who we are, more even than what we sell. My clients had better know how much I care, how real I am, and believe I'm working every day to help them fulfill their goals and dreams. If they truly believe that, then how can they say no to me?

Ten years ago, I was fighting for an account against two national, name-brand banks. The potential client was one I had a real affinity for: Local 22, the Philadelphia Firefighters Union, twenty-three thousand strong. We had been trying to win their business for a couple years with no luck; if you're trying to get that sort of account, there's a lot of politics involved. (*Lots.*) But even though they weren't clients, we stayed in touch with the leadership. Good guys. Now, the union had opened the bid, attracting the interest of multiple suitors. The day we appeared at the union office to make our pitch, the big bankers pulled up in a limo, all the way from New York. I was waiting with my partner in the union office's reception area. The bankers entered, in suits that cost at least a couple grand each. Do I really have to point out that their hair was slicked back? They nodded at us, we at them.

The bankers went first. When they came out a half-hour later, they departed in the waiting limo, and headed (I presume) back to New York City.

I noticed that one of them had mistakenly left behind his presentation. It was beautifully bound, just about the most professional-looking dossier you could dream up. Ours was fine and professional but not sleek like theirs. Ours had been done on an office printer.

Now it was our turn to pitch the union. By the time we finished, a half-hour later, I thought we had nailed it. To be honest, the fact that I had been burned and I was a former volunteer firefighter didn't hurt. I figured a lot of the guys we were pitching respected that.

Immediately afterward, I picked up my son Matt at home and we drove the seven hours to North Carolina where he was starting college at High Point University. We got there in the early evening and went straight to Target to pick up some things for his dorm room. As we loaded up the Suburban, my phone rang. It was Rich from the firefighters union.

"Brian, we got a problem," he said. The vote was tied between us and the big bank that had presented right before us. "Both of you have impressive portfolios. I'm not sure we see enough difference between you guys to decide based on that. What would you do?"

"Rich, buddy, you heard what we had to say. You heard what they had to say. Maybe their portfolio will work out better, maybe ours will. Right now, before you choose, it's impossible to say. It's not a perfect science. So, yeah, I see your predicament. You're going to have to look elsewhere to make the decision. You saw when they came in, right? A limo from New York. To Philly. You saw that gorgeous report they had with them. That cost something. Who do you think pays for all that, in the end?"

There was silence on his end.

"We're giving you steak, Rich. They're giving you sizzle. You gotta decide whether you want to eat steak or smell sizzle. That's the best analogy I can give you."

A couple of hours later, Rich called back. "Your line worked! I used it! We're going with the steak!"

(The line isn't original to me—yeah, a bit of a cliché—but thanks, Rich.)

I don't pretend that integrity in business is so unusual, though I do think the bigger you get, the harder it is to achieve or maintain. Harder, but not impossible. Everything else being equal, I believe you're better off in a small- to medium-size company, whether as client or employee. The owners are simply more involved. The decisions they make are more connected to everyone in the company, not just the next tier of managers. I have a feeling for all our employees. During the 2008 global financial meltdown, our firm did not lay off a single employee, did not suspend anyone's pay, did not even forego bonuses. How many big companies did that? How many big banks? Very few—because it's just not something they worry about. Not long ago, Deutsche Bank announced they were planning to lay off seven to ten thousand workers globally. You know what all the other big banks were feeling about Deutsche's announcement? Gratitude. *Thank you, Deutsche Bank. Danke schön.* Because once the first big-name place does it, it gives cover to all the others. *It's the fiscally prudent thing for our shareholders, as our competitors are forced to consolidate in the same blah blah blah....*

Here's a question: After the 2008 financial collapse and the smaller 2013 one, after so many of those big financial institutions made "necessary" cuts like suspending 401(k)-matching programs because they were "fiscally imprudent to maintain at the moment"...now that things are stronger economically, and have been for the last six years, how many of those big firms re-started those matching programs, which exist to help their rank and file?

What puzzles and upsets me is how ethical conflicts become so blatant that they normalize hypocrisy and questionable behavior. An SEC official leaves his position to be the head of compliance for a big bank. Is he or she there to help them navigate and abide by a thicket of ever-changing government regulations—or to instruct them on how to evade the scrutiny of people who do what he or she once did? If the latter, isn't there something wrong with that?

Or here's an example from a totally different realm: When I went for a colonoscopy at a local surgery center, a place with a great reputation, I noticed the overwhelming purpleness of the room—purple rug, purple seat covers, purple pens on the doctor's desk. The doctor told me how the procedure would go: I would be under sedation for maybe twenty minutes, during which time he would perform the colonoscopy, then I would be in recovery, where he would come talk with me. When the surgery was done, I waited in another room, also bathed in purple. The doctor and the anesthesiologist entered. The doctor, a fellow I know and respect and who seems good at his job, told me that everything looked good except for some irritation in my esophagus, which could lead to acid reflux. "So I'm going to prescribe some medication for you to take," he told me. "Nexium." He handed me a prescription—and it dawned on me that so much of the purple around the room was Nexium-branded.

"Wait, doc, hold on a second," I said. I was slightly groggy from the anesthesia, but I wasn't blind. "Is there a reason the chairs are purple and the rug is purple and your pens are purple—and I'm getting what I'm guessing is a purple pill? That's just a coincidence?"

Behind the doctor, the anesthesiologist was—how do I put it— laughing his ass off.

I have no beef with Nexium. I'm not suggesting it was unnecessary for me, or that it doesn't work. I'm saying that I don't want my doctor recommending that I take a purple pill and presenting the decision as if it's the embodiment of objectivity when he's deep enough on their payroll that his office looks like a shrine to purple.

Our firm's simple rule: No one takes gifts from anyone—not from a group, not from an individual, no one. No meal, no drink, no gum, nothing. If a client is in my office or on the phone and I'm recommending that he buy a certain stock or financial instrument, I do not want him wondering for even a millisecond that maybe it's because the person who benefits most from the transaction is a guy who gave Mary Ann and me VIP tickets to an Eagles game.

We do no advertising. None. One hundred percent of our business is by word of mouth. We don't run seminars. That's not so much a stand for ethical behavior as it is a mark of confidence and a reminder to not let our foot off the gas. I believe that if you do what you're good at and you do what you say you'll do, you win, every time. *Our single most important selling point is the authentic conversation we have with the potential client.* I believe our philosophy is so sound that people will actually understand it. Can you imagine that?! If they don't understand what we're recommending or why they're holding what they're holding, then we sit with them until they do, however long it takes. Some clients want to know where I have my own money—a legitimate question, just like asking your doctor if he or she would make this or that decision about a procedure if they were considering it for their child or their own self. Always a smart hypothetical. Some clients don't quite understand and get outright suspicious if I suggest putting them in something I'm not in. "Sheila, I'm in my fifties and I own a business, which is far and away my biggest asset," I told one client. "You're sixty-seven, retired, and cash is your largest asset. There's no way you should be in what I'm in." If we can't help them to understand, then there's something wrong with what we're doing or with us. And we don't deserve their business.

You can't have self-belief without integrity.

(Well, you can, but that would mean you believe in someone without integrity.)

* * *

It's *my* life. I wanted the decisions about it to be mine—mostly, anyway. I wanted to do it my way. Brian Jr. once asked me when exactly I present the physical contract to the customer to "close the sale" of our working relationship. "Never," I told him. "I never make them sign a contract.

I'm not selling them anything. They're either going to use our services or not. I always assume they're going to come on board, based on how I've treated them and what they can hear and see that I do for them. I never say, 'Hey, you need to sign with us today.' If they're hearing what I'm telling them, we don't need a contract. And if they're not hearing what I say, so be it. Pressuring them does nobody any good."

If you believe in yourself, then you hold yourself completely accountable. At our firm, we forbid anyone to assign blame to others. I once worked at a giant insurance firm where my boss's bonus—and mine, too—was tied to how many people we hired. It didn't matter if the hires were good at what they did, or even if they stayed on; it was all about your hiring numbers. Not only is that unethical, in my opinion, and defeating to good work, but what a great way to deflect blame! *Don't look at me, what about any of the twenty-five new hires from this past quarter? Take your pick!* (I quit the firm.) Once, I was at a meeting at another firm and someone explained that he didn't have the promised documents ready for me because, he lamented, "My assistant screwed up."

I was so incensed by the comment that when I returned to our office, I repeated the incident to everyone and said simply, "If I hear something like that come out of anybody's mouth in this office, they're gone." I knew the character of my staff, so I knew it was extremely unlikely that that would happen. But given my anger, I wanted to make sure I was on record.

Wherever you are on the ladder, you're responsible. If something goes wrong underneath you, you're responsible. If you didn't manage the situation correctly or didn't teach someone correctly, you're responsible. There's a distinction I often use, a line I quote courtesy of the brilliant Nido Qubein, whom I also consider a friend. In the Q&As after speeches I sometimes give about the state of the financial services industry, one question comes up more than any other: "How do you train your employees?"

Crediting Nido, I like to reply, "I don't train my employees. I *educate* them. And if you don't think there's a difference between training and education, ask yourself: when your kids are in high school, do you want them to go through sex education or sex training?"

You have to educate your people not just about What and How, but Why. Why they're doing something. Why it matters. Why they matter. So everyone knows their responsibilities.

* * *

My personal life influenced my business life. There's nothing special about that statement except that, in my case, much of what I learned about the world and people and myself should be seen through the lens of what happened to me on October 24, 1981, and the reaction to that event.

Here are a few lessons that are as applicable to me as a businessman as they are to me as a human being:

-Have no agenda.

Maybe it was reading people's eyes as they unabashedly stared at me, or the perspective I developed while "hiding" behind a mask myself, that accelerated my understanding of people. And nearly everyone, it seemed to me, had an agenda. That didn't make the person bad, but it did tell me that the exchanges I had were always influenced, though often silently, by the other person's overriding goal (maybe mine, too, to be honest). God knows, the agenda is generally more naked in business transactions, or whenever money's involved, than in other areas of life. I decided to be the one *without* an agenda, if only to set myself apart. Charles Darwin might have said that I must have thought I could gain more by not having an agenda, so that was my agenda. And sure, I did think operating agenda-less could help me—in self-esteem, in appealing to others, in professional success. Most of all, though, it was in the pleasure and satisfaction I derive from doing things for their own sake, like taking extra time to talk with all the often overlooked people who help me in a given day—the hotel maid, the cabbie, the busboy, the doorman. I've seen people for whom over-tipping, or even average tipping, or the occasional kind gesture—spending emotion and warmth for a brief conversation, an inquiry or two to make someone feel recognized and respected—is "a waste of time." If you're not making money, they believe, you're squandering it. If you're not winning, you're losing. To me, that's a sad, false, zero-sum view of the world. A business acquaintance once remarked that the people I spent time conversing with at the hotel I frequent in Los Angeles couldn't "help" me.

"You're right, they're not helping me," I said. "But they're helping me."

How does this philosophy influence how I conduct my professional business? I start with the principle that by helping others I *am* helping myself, even if it's not always obvious. It means doing things that, at least at first, seem counter to my "best interest." For example, there's an array of options I can offer my clients. My job is to help him or her choose the one that best suits their needs even if that choice doesn't pay me the highest commission. In my office we look at the track record, expenses, and performance of any financial product before recommending it to clients.

I know there are brokers who avoid the lower commission options, no matter how sterling a particular product's record might be. So many brokers put their customers into products that have the benefit *for the broker* of paying a high management fee. How many people can they rope in? A lot, apparently. I've witnessed this practice in larger firms.

If I were in it for me first, there are numerous choices where I would receive more in commissions. But those choices would then have to perform unrealistically well, year after year, to be worth it for the client, even as I would make more money, at least in the first couple years.

Instead of trying just to make more money, I want to make my client happy. If I do that, he or she will want to stay with me, or do even more business with me, or tell friends about me.

And there you have it: I lied. Darwin was right. Because I just confessed to an agenda. If they win, I win. Success through long-term altruism.

-Form as many relationships, with as many types of people, as possible.

The best thing about being a firefighter was the camaraderie. Forging relationships with different types of people. Understanding people better. It wasn't just the fire service that taught me that; the bonding of firefighting was just more intense. I'm sure the same is true for those in combat together.

But we don't need extreme situations to form deep bonds. Every single person is worthy of respect and dignity, no matter where they come from or who they are. How can it be that we actually have to write or say that? How do we not automatically all live by that? Where do people learn to treat certain people as less than who they are? What must someone think of him or herself to do that? Every conversation I have with cabbies and Uber and Lyft drivers tells me they're doing their best to make a living. A lot of them work seven days a week. Most of them work more than just that one job. Most of them have families they're trying to support. Some of them are going through the immigration process. Some of them have their families here but still send money to people they left back home. I talk with them because I want them to know there are people out there who respect and admire what they're doing.

I do my best to treat people this way for three reasons: the person feels good, I feel good, and I wanted to model behavior for my kids as they were growing up. (I should be clear: my patience with humanity is hardly boundless. As Sonny Leuzzi, one of my very best friends, says, "When you're a douchebag, you're a douchebag.")

Of course, my kids already had a good idea about how to behave around people who didn't have it all; hey, they grew up with a dad who had a burnt face. That was normal to them. In fact, for a long time, they didn't even realize there was anything unusual about my face. That really only happened when they started playing youth sports, and at some point they each asked me why I didn't look like the other dads. The question touched and saddened me because I knew that they probably hadn't thought to ask the question; a teammate would have noticed me on the sidelines or in the stands and asked Brian Jr. or Matt or Katie about it. Maybe my kids got asked about it by friends in school when they were younger but weren't ready to ask me.

Because of my circumstance, my kids got a valuable head start on some of their contemporaries in accepting people for who they are. It didn't matter what you looked like, what religion you were, how much money you made, where you went to school, what your SAT score was, how well you spoke or dressed, if you had a profession or "just" a job, or occasionally no job at all. To them you were a person. I think that's the single biggest thing I've tried to give them—that Mary Ann and I have tried to give them. The world of people they can and do befriend and genuinely interact with is vast.

-Do business only with people you enjoy being around—colleagues or customers.

Okay, it's hard to do that with *every* customer. But if my life post-fire taught me just one thing, it's that time is precious, and if you waste it on people you don't enjoy being around, well, don't blame them.

* * *

If you're good with who you are, decisions are easier. Your sleep is less fitful. My success in business would not have happened if I didn't believe there was a right way to do things. If others don't think I'm doing it the right way, there's only so much I can do to convince them. Put another way: that's *their* problem.

A few years ago, my friend Tom Stewart, who worked for Verizon, had colleagues who were getting early retirement buyouts and needed someone to manage their assets. At lunch one day, Tom told these friends that his buddy (me) "does this kind of thing" and that they should talk to me. I got a call from his friend Joe, a representative of sorts for the group, and he came to our office. I heard his concerns, shared our philosophy, and promised I'd do some preliminary retirement calculating and projections for him and each person in the group. By the end of the meeting, he seemed to like what he had heard, but he told me that he and the group were speaking with other firms, too, which I encourage. Joe reported back to his co-workers on his conversations with us and other firms, and recommended that they choose us to manage their assets. He himself had decided to go with us. Some of the guys contacted me directly, asking for more extensive calculations about their particular situation, before they made a decision. I put a lot of work into it, as we do with all clients and potential clients, collected a lot of pertinent data, and went to the homes of a few of them. Over the next two weeks, ten of the Verizon gang, including Joe and my friend Tom, joined, a great piece of business for us.

Not all of them did, though. One who didn't was the person who had asked for the most extensive projections, by far. His name was also Tom. (I know a lot of Toms.) One morning, after days of his asking me for more and more info, Tom called and said, "I'm really sorry, Brian." He said they were going with a name-brand New York bank because his wife was "a little more comfortable with their approach."

Now, I hate losing. For me, everything is about the hunt. Frankly, I don't get all that much joy from the victory (except if it's the Philadelphia Eagles winning the Super Bowl). Professional victory, I mean; I know enough to appreciate the "victories" and beautiful moments in my personal life. But in business, I am more motivated by not losing than by winning. Losing bothers me much more than winning gives me a rush.

And I especially hate losing to the "big guys"—any of the household-name banks. For one, they may have particular stocks and deals that their overseers pressure and incentivize them to sell. These deals may not be in the client's best interest.

For another, I can't imagine that the big bank's system or philosophy is better than ours. Our philosophy is based on efficiency, diversification, and cost. That's it. Make sure your (transaction) costs are reasonable (low) enough that the portfolio can absorb the cost of itself. There's a lot more to it than that, of course, but there's no proof like results. We've grown every single year since we opened in 1991, and even recorded some of our best years (2008, 2009, 2010) when most of the rest of the market was hemorrhaging.

There's a third reason I don't like to lose to the big firms, though I know why we sometimes do: some firms, in order to win business, overpromise, plain and simple. They paint you a picture of a world that does not exist but that you wish could. Until he was unmasked, Bernie Madoff tapped into this desire beautifully. Beware of big firms that make projections that have little to do with reality. Then—surprise!—they underdeliver. And of course it's the market's fault. The economy's fault.

Congress's fault. China's fault. It's always someone or something else. It can never be the big powerhouse firm and the way they do things because they're household names, right? We get more referrals during down markets than at any other time. Why? The big-name broker is suddenly not as quick to return your calls about why things didn't pan out the way he or she (over)promised.

Back to Tom: I was a little bummed to lose his business and that of his few Verizon buddies who also went with the big bank. I felt we were the best place for them. I knew we had made the best presentation we could.

I also firmly believe that the way you handle yourself in difficult moments comes back to you, in good ways or bad. *Always.* I never burn a bridge. (I would rush to put it out, though. Okay, sorry for that one.)

I thanked Tom for his call informing me about his decision and wished him and his wife the best. I told him if anything changed and he needed to consult with me, especially given how well I now understood his finances, he should call, no charge, no hard feelings.

Part of me expected to hear nothing from Tom ever again.

Another part of me thought I would because unless the big bank's plan wildly surpassed what we would have done for him, then why wouldn't you go with the firm that handled themselves like we did? A firm that knew who it was, that wasn't going to tell you anything but what they believed was best for you, and that could honestly deliver on it?

A year later. It was late January, not long after we had completed most of our year-end portfolio reviews, and the phone rang. I could see who it was.

"Hey, Tom," I said.

After we exchanged pleasantries, he said, "So I just got off the phone with a few of my Verizon pals who are your clients. About how well their portfolio is doing. I'm down six percent. What's going on?"

In that particular market, you'd have to work practically a reverse-miracle to be down six percent. But nobody is in the mood for wisecracks when they're losing money. "I can't say, Tom. I don't know what the people at your bank have you in."

"Could I fax you my statements and you could maybe look at them?"

"Sure, Tom. If you're down six percent in this climate, we should definitely take a look."

When you're troubled enough to make that call to me, you're already committed. You want us. You just need validation that your thinking is correct. You're pretty much there.

I didn't resent Tom for doubting me the first time. As long I stayed true to myself, good things would come. Redemption has a way of taking care of itself.

Tom sent me his statements. His broker hadn't done anything wildly unjustified, based on the information that Tom had shared with me the previous year.

"Your guy didn't do anything wrong, Tom," I said when I called back. "He put together a portfolio he thought would work out and it just hasn't. I don't know what else to tell you."

Tom and his wife moved all their business to us, as did the remaining holdouts. That was fifteen years ago. For the first three or four years of the relationship, Tom and his wife Cathy were consistently—among the thousand-plus clients we serve—the ones who demanded *the* most detailed review, the most painstaking analysis of how they were doing, even as they were doing extremely well. (For those years when we didn't quite meet projections, we were always close.) Each year Tom and Cathy wanted to sit with me, and Cathy always had an armful of folders.

For the last many years and counting, when they come to my office for the year-end review, they no longer bring anything with them—no folders, no paperwork, nothing. For a while, I couldn't help a little ribbing. "Cathy, where are your folders? Did you forget them?"

She always smiles. "We can't complain," she says.

* * *

The *carpe diem* philosophy I embraced after my accident helped shape my investing philosophy in some ways, yet I consider myself more conservative than a lot of financial advisors out there. I split my goals between the present and the future. People often sacrifice one for the other, but it's a balancing act. For example, I have savings goals for myself—once I hit those, though, I spend my money. I see no reason for over-saving. *People say overspending is a sin. Isn't over-saving a sin, too?*

You don't know what's going to happen tomorrow, so be prudent.

You don't know what's going to happen tomorrow, so enjoy.

They make equal sense to me.

Yet so many people are spooked into over-saving. Cliff, a client, once said to me, "I want to give you a lump sum of my money for a few years so you can help me map out when I can buy a new house."

As his financial manager, I knew his situation. "Cliff, don't give me the money," I told him. "I don't want it. Because you can buy a house *now*. Your financial standing is strong. Find the house you want, make yourself happy *now*. You don't have to save for another three years to do that. But thanks for the offer."

I have clients whose admirable values obstruct them from seeing what's best. For example: One woman, Anne, who grew up during the Depression, has been a client since 1993. I love her like a second mom. She's a wonderful person. Her husband died when he was in his early fifties. Anne has been living off the same monthly dollar amount she did in 1996, when she retired. Every year, when we review her portfolio, I tell her she needs to go spend some money.

"I want to leave some for the kids," she says.

"They don't need anything," I tell her. They don't. Her kids are also my clients. "Spend it, do something. It's okay."

"My husband and I saved all this money and I can't enjoy it without him," she says.

Since I can't fight that line of argument, I tell her, "Fair enough. But maybe you should do something with the kids. Maybe take everybody on vacation?"

I'm not there just to advise my clients on making good investments but also to let them know ways they can spend it and enjoy life more, when they may be depriving themselves for no good reason.

* * *

It's good I started my own business. Though I worked under people for a while, I would have chafed at it had I done it much longer. They wouldn't have enjoyed it either.

I wanted to do things my way. I love the entrepreneurial spirit of following your instinct and trying to bring something to life. When Kevin Nicholson and I started out, we worked with a property and casualty agency; we were basically their internal life insurance, benefits, and investment division. Our office was the back of the house where the agency was based, conveniently located close to where Kevin and I each lived. Our office was really only big enough for one person, so we had to manage. We shared a landline. "Hey, you making a call right now? Because I need to make one...." Pretty pathetic. But you do what you have to. And with few clients and not much cash flow, we learned to keep our expenses very low.

It was a big deal when we could finally rent two parts of the office—I took a room on the third floor, Kevin one on the first. Now we had our own phones. We would page each other if we had a question.

We trusted each other to do what each did best. He could go deep in the weeds on the financial stuff in a way that would not have made me happy. My strength is in getting people to talk about what they want for their life and how we can help make that happen.

We've been business partners for twenty-eight years and counting.

No one will mistake my hometown of Levittown for the Main Line. It's straight blue-collar, hard-working, no-nonsense. Coming from a home where eight kids shared two bedrooms, where I shared a bed with my brother, was all to my advantage. It forged discipline in me. And I never forget what it takes to get where I got.

My accident made me grow up faster. It made me understand who I was and what I wanted. It made me know what and who I was willing to put up with. Since I have my own business, I make sure that two kinds of people never got hired: the Lazy and the Cheap. I have no time for either. If you have your health and there's no other significant obstacle, why would you ever be lazy?

And having my own business meant I wasn't going to "cut corners" ethically the way some places do. I didn't want to let small things slide, because small things eventually become big things. I wouldn't let us win at all costs, much as I hate to lose. In fact, I find the phrase "win at all costs" one of the saddest out there. *You simply cannot Win At All Costs. It's a logical impossibility. It's a statement that eats itself. If you have paid all the costs—damaging relationships, breaking laws, breaking your own ethical code—then you have lost. It doesn't matter what it says on the scoreboard or your balance sheet.*

CHAPTER 10:

Stock Up on Foxholes

True friends say good things behind your
back and bad things to your face.
—Anonymous

I can't say that every important lesson that helped me live a meaningful life was "thanks" to my surviving a fire. By the time you make it to age seventeen, a lot of who you are—probably most—is set. Technically, I may have been a junior firefighter, but I had been fighting fires for more than a year and a half before my accident and had by then fully embraced the "first responder" mentality—never content just to observe a situation but always *assessing* it, trying to spot quickly where help was needed, how to make things better. My kids will tell you that this urge isn't always a wonderful thing. My inclination to swoop in and do something, anything, as soon as a problem presents itself is sometimes unwelcome because the best plan may involve my *not* helping, or letting someone else take the lead, or simply letting things play out.

Still, once a first responder, always a first responder. And the feeling is taken to another level when you serve with others, like a company of firefighters, and you know what you are capable of as a team.

At its heart, *the first responder mentality rests on two beliefs: The world is eternally wounded, and people are always in need of help.* It is this mentality, along with something that Lester Rosen liked to say—"your goal in life is not to be better than anyone else but to be better than your previous self"—that have influenced how I try to lead my professional and personal lives. Of course, once you go through something like I did, and you're fortunate to come out the other side, your every day is shaped by the combination of massive gratitude, perspective, and flat-out urgency that you feel. The question I always try to ask myself is, "What can I do to be better?" And while I'm trying to answer that question, there's always time to pick up the phone and say to someone in need, "Are you alright?" We always say we're busy, busy...are we, really? As busy as we say? Maybe we say it to give ourselves a break. Psychologically, when someone hears that we're busy, they pull back. At a conference I attended, one speaker put it beautifully. "If someone asks if you're busy, don't respond 'Yes, I am.' Instead say, 'I'm never too busy for an opportunity.'" I love that. It's the best possible answer for both parties.

Why am I so driven to succeed? Is it gratitude for getting a second chance at life? No. It all comes down to fear. Not fear of failure; that doesn't scare me. But fear of missing out on the opportunity to make someone's life better, or to make myself better (so that I'm even better equipped to help). Lots of things fade with time, but the opportunity to help someone, even if just a bit, never goes away until you're dead. It's there, so why not try to do it? Is that "driven"? I just think I appreciate the fight. Maybe that's one of the reasons I wanted to become a volunteer in the fire service. We're called fire*fighters*.

I have a friend who called me one Tuesday, mid-morning, at a particularly troubled time in his life. He could have called his brother, who lived much closer to him, but he didn't. I told my admin to cancel my meetings for the rest of the day and I drove out to my friend's and helped get him through his situation. I'm not telling you this to pat myself on the back for how I acted; most people, in similar circumstances, would do more or less what I did.

No, I tell it because it meant so much to me that I was the one that my friend called.

Is it a burden to be the person that someone calls when that someone doesn't know where to turn? Sure—if you consider life itself a burden. What could be a greater reward and honor than being that person for another human being? Or for many human beings?

* * *

My great friends Sonny and Tina, along with Mary Ann and I, have a name for it: "foxhole people." Your truest of friends, the kind you can call at three in the morning and they don't judge, they just drop everything. Somebody whose trust you never question or even question questioning. Someone who has your best interests at heart always, not some version of your best interest so long as it coincides with theirs. Who isn't there for you just when things go bad, but also three weeks later or four months later, after the crowds paying respects in your living room have gone, after the local deli has stopped delivering daily food platters prepaid by a friend or family member so you wouldn't have to prepare meals in the first days of shock following a tragedy.

A foxhole friend is also someone with whom you can be completely unfiltered when you need to. There is no chance they will mistake what you say for something it isn't because they know your heart.

You're lucky if you come through life with a foxhole friend. You're lucky if you can count them on one hand. If you have four or three or two true friends like that, consider yourself lucky. When you look back on your life, if you had "just" one foxhole friend, consider yourself lucky. I mean it. Because of what they mean to you, that's all you need.

I tell my kids: *your job in life is to be the foxhole person for as many people as you can.*

I've made that my goal. You should want to make people open up around you. To want you to be the one they turn to. And not just the person to call in a pinch. The one to call when they've got a story to tell, or a joke, or suddenly their 11:30 cancelled and they've got time for lunch and you're the one they want to grab it with. On a golf outing, yours is the foursome they want to complete. If you can think of just one person who fills that role for you, great. That's all you need to hope for.

When you find your people, you know. And they're always out there—in a new class, at a new job, at your health club, wherever. If you're spending lots of time with people whom you have no interest being foxhole friends with, maybe you're misusing your time.

Mary Ann is my number one foxhole person. She met me when I was the burned guy and she saw through the mask and the grafts, when many people in my life couldn't. Lots of my firefighter buddies could see through it, and so could Mary Ann. It helps if the person you're married to or partnered with is on your very short list of people you most trust.

My aim is that everyone smiles when they know they're going to see me, because they know it's going to be a good encounter—warm, funny, maybe some trash-talking, always memorable and positive. They should always know where it's coming from. I'm not saying I always succeed. But I want to be somebody that people want in their lives, in one way or another. I want people to know that they can call on me and rely on me. I aim to do that for so many people, one of them will say to me one day, "Dude, you need a bigger foxhole."

* * *

It was a Tuesday night, so there weren't many people at the bar. It was probably a year since I'd left the hospital. I had my mask on, as always. Johnny Glasson had stopped by the house earlier. "Let's go grab a beer," he said. He didn't say it like he was asking. He *announced*, "Let's go grab a beer. Irishman's."

The Irishman's was a bar a few minutes away. I was happy to be there, to be out of the house. I was especially happy to be with Johnny, who was a little larger than life to me and to many others in our circle, and to all the people who had experienced fires he had helped fight. Johnny told Jack, the owner and also the bartender that day, that he wanted a Budweiser for himself and a small glass of beer for me. I felt almost at ease.

Further down the bar, two men in their twenties were whispering to each other and occasionally glancing at me. One tried to hide a laugh, then the other laughed, not even bothering to hide it. Johnny noticed them, too. I saw his shoulders draw back.

"Johnny, it's okay," I told him. "It's no big deal." This wasn't my first time among people who had never seen someone like me, or seen a guy in a mask. Though you'd think a guy in a mask was not *that* shocking. I mean, seriously. I had kind of acclimated to the reaction, for better or worse, even though the predictability of some people, in some situations, disappointed me. "I'm used to it," I told Johnny, a half-lie.

Johnny hadn't heard a word I'd said.

"Excuse me a minute," he said in my direction, in a voice that was scary calm. Johnny Glasson was not someone who got rattled. He stood, walked to where the bar curved, leaned into the two men, then grabbed the closer one by the collar. Johnny said something to him in a low voice. I couldn't make it out. I assumed it was something like, *You making fun of my buddy over here?* Or, *You have a problem with my friend?*

"Oh no, no, no," said the guy whose collar had been shortened by Johnny's grip. The guy was in full retreat, denying whatever it was that Johnny had accused him of. But his body language reeked of—I don't know how else to put it—arrogance and guilt. Johnny yanked the guy down from his bar stool and dragged him across the floor of the bar, like a human mop, until, with a final swift tug, Johnny drove the guy's head into the large beer freezer near our corner of the bar. The freezer glass split from the impact.

Suddenly the floor was covered in blood. Johnny, who had not yet let go of his catch, half-picked him up, dragged him toward the back exit door, pushed it open, and slid the guy into the back alley. Johnny calmly shut the door behind him, walked back over to me, sat down, and took a sip from his thirty-two-ounce Bud, like we had just paused from talking about the Flyers or the weather.

I sat there with my glass of beer, not knowing what to think. It happened so fast.

The guy's friend, equally stunned, called out, "You gotta call an ambulance!" He disappeared out the back to check on his friend.

Jack walked out from behind the bar toward the back, opened the door, looked out at what I assumed was the bleeding victim and his buddy, returned to the bar, picked up the phone, and called 911.

A few minutes later, sirens. The police, an ambulance. Suddenly the back alley was filled with commotion. I tried to sip my glass of beer, but it was hard. A cop entered through the back door. It was someone Johnny and I both recognized—John Schwab, a member of our volunteer fire department. (I know a lot of Johns.) He approached us.

"Johnny, what happened?" asked John the cop.

"I don't know, Schwab. I don't know what happened," said Johnny, and from his tone of voice, his confidence and authority, I practically believed myself that he *didn't* know, though I had seen everything unfold right in front of my eyes just minutes before. "All of a sudden this kid went berserk. He fucking hit his head on the cooler, then he went out back. That's all I know."

Schwab looked at him. He took an extra beat before he spoke. "You're kidding me, right?"

The guy's friend, who at some point had returned from the alley and now reappeared in the bar, pointed at Johnny and started yelling. "*He beat up my friend! This guy*—he beat up my friend!"

Schwab studied Johnny some more.

"What do you want me to tell you?" said Johnny, addressing Schwab and ignoring the yelling stranger. "That's all I know happened."

"This guy beat up my friend!" the guy's buddy repeated. It was interesting to me that his voice and face were so animated, yet his body remained perfectly still, except for his finger wagging and pointing at Johnny. Then again, there was a neighborhood cop with a sidearm just feet from him.

Schwab turned to Jack. "What happened here?"

Jack shrugged. "I don't know," he said. "I didn't see a thing."

Schwab looked at him for a few seconds, then a few more at Johnny, then me. He raised his eyebrow. "All right," he said. "I don't think I need to do anything about this."

No one ever brought it up again, except at parties, when Johnny or I got a couple in us. The guy who had laughed at me and ended up bleeding in the alley got stitched up at the nearby hospital. Nobody ever saw him or his buddy again.

I'm not cheerleading violence as a way of resolving differences. I'm just describing one way to spot a foxhole person.

*   *   *

I'll repeat myself: ***There can be no success, no real-life success, period, without attention to people.*** One of the sayings in my business is, "They don't care how much you know until they know how much you care." Somehow I figured that out early. Even in the hospital, though I was the one in deep trouble, I knew that no one else's life just stopped for mine. Their troubles didn't magically all go away or suddenly stop piling on. For those close to me, their lives got worse, too, because of what happened to me, and in fact their sense of helplessness in some ways grew more even than mine. After all, once I walked out of the burn unit on my own power, my sense of helplessness dropped significantly. My mother says the time I was in the burn unit were the worst thirty-seven days of her life, and I don't pretend that Day Thirty-Eight and beyond were automatically wonderful for her.

While I was hospitalized, there was a real danger of turning inward, and I had to fight that by looking outward, to others. For example: My oldest brother and frequent tormentor, Ed, worked near the burn center and visited me almost every day at lunchtime. One day he told me, "Listen, Bri, I won't be down here the next couple days because I've got a court date. Don't say anything to anyone. They need to be here with you. But I wanted you to know why I won't be here."

I had the tube in, so I just nodded. I knew that my brother was going to attend the trial of a man who had stabbed him two years earlier. Ed had gotten into a fight outside a bar, a fight started by a disgruntled drunk who mistook Ed for someone else, then stabbed him even as Ed tried to calm the guy. The guy's lawyer was painting it as something more one-sided than that.

A few hours after Ed left my bedside, my father visited. I reached for my pad and pen. *Better go help out Ed*, I wrote, defying my brother's instructions. I explained, with more scribbling, about Ed's court date. I had enough people looking after me. Dad could miss a day.

The next day, my dad walked into the courtroom and sat in the gallery. When Ed saw him, he was shocked and a little confused because nobody knew about the court appearance but me. During a break in the trial, Ed approached Dad in the hall. "What are you doing here? You should be with Brian."

"He wrote me a note to come down here because you were going through this and no one would be here," Dad told Ed.

My brother got miffed at me, I heard, but I bet deep down he was happy to have Dad there. A couple days later, Ed came by for his lunch-hour visit. "I thought I told you not to say anything," he said.

As much as I could grin through the mask, I grinned. I did what I did because it was the right thing. Because everyone needs support, and on that day, he needed it more than I did.

And okay, sure, part of me did it because it was my big brother and, you know, screw you, Ed.

* * *

After I got out of the burn unit, I gradually became more expressive and emotive. I felt better able to connect with people, and they with me. Being emotionally open, I realized, allows you to connect with people across a range of backgrounds and experiences.

I'm more open with my kids than some of my brothers and sisters were with theirs, and I think it's rubbed off on my siblings in a positive way. Ed, for example, was never big on "sharing," be it his worries, his stories, his past, his affection. There can be a standoffish quality in my first family; we didn't grow up hugging or expressing our love for each other. Yeah, every family has a style, but some styles just don't help as many people as other styles do. Judgmental, and true. I had to *learn* to not keep it in. A lot of that I owe to Mary Ann and the much more openly affectionate way her parents and family were around one another. Now I'm that way. I'm credited with introducing hugging to some of my siblings and their families. I started hugging my parents more after the accident. I became more expressive. That gradually filtered to other members of the family. But damn: ***Must it really take something terrible like a fire to teach emotionally closed people to open up?***

Nothing made me happier than to hear my nephew, Ed Jr., tell me about a Christmas morning at his home one year when my father, not a warm and fuzzy man, hugged him and his siblings. "I was like, Holy shit!" Ed Jr. told me. "I can't believe this is happening!"

* * *

It's not just my kids who think I go overboard with my first responder tendency. My friends will tweak me about it, too. Once, while golfing on the first day of April with my good friend Phil Ring, he hit his ball out of bounds and went looking for it at the edge of a marsh. I saw him searching—then tumble backward and disappear. I raced over in the cart. Finally, he staggered up the incline from the marsh. "Shit! I got bit by a fucking snake!" he yelled.

My first responder tendency shifted immediately into gear and I drove the cart practically into the marsh to get to him.

"Come on! Are you able to get into the cart yourself? Let's go!"

"It was a big snake!" said Phil, laboring. "Big! Snake!"

"Get in, get in! Let's get you to the nearest hospital—"

"April Fool's," he said.

Phil was lucky I was sitting in the golf cart and not standing next to him with a nine-iron or he'd be dead right now. He will never play another April Fool's joke on me as long as we're both alive.

Still, it was funny. I probably had it coming.

CHAPTER 11:

Imagine It's Worse

The only sure thing about luck is that it will change.
—Wilson Mizner

My first, "original" family taught me some valuable lessons about people, including one that many of us keep forgetting, much as we try not to: it could always be worse. Because I'm from a blended family, tragically blended.

While I am one of eight kids, my mother gave birth to only five of us. In the spring of 1959, it was Kathleen, Ed and Kevin, with Renee on the way. I wouldn't arrive for another five years. In the middle of June, 1959, my Uncle Bill—Dad's brother—bought a new station wagon. He brought it home, and my Aunt Marie and their kids, all six of them, piled in, the kids in the back two rows, the youngest—six months old—on someone's lap in the middle. This was long before seat-belt and child-oriented safety rules. It would be their first ride all together in the new car.

It would also be their last. A drunk driver ran a stop sign. Aunt Marie died the next day, never regaining consciousness. Uncle Bill was in a coma until he passed away three months later.

The six kids got split up. The older girls, Patty and Marie, went to live with Grandma Anna, Dad's mom, but after a year it was clear that she couldn't care for two young girls, so they came to live with us. The three boys—Billy, Richie, and Joey—went to live with another aunt and uncle, though Billy eventually left them and joined us. Annie, a baby at the time of the crash, was taken in by another uncle. In the two to three years after the crash, our family went from four kids to seven. Marie became our oldest, Billy my sometime protector, Patty the closest. When I showed up a year later, I had seven brothers and sisters. I never thought of some as cousins or less legit siblings.

That's how it was.

*   *   *

We were the lucky ones. That's how we looked at it.

We weren't well off—but suddenly there were three more mouths to feed, so Mom and Dad had to find a way. And look what Uncle Bill and Aunt Marie's kids had to deal with on top of all that—loss, sadness, a sense of displacement. It could always be worse.

If we dared to think we had it bad, we knew that the Glassons, who lived a dozen blocks away, had it worse. There were *thirteen* Glasson kids. Mr. Glasson died of Guillain-Barré syndrome when Kevin was twelve. Mrs. Glasson had multiple sclerosis. They were on Social Security disability. Throughout their house you walked on the burlap backing of the carpet. Everything's relative, right?

My brother and sister have type 1 diabetes. So does Matt. It's possible my dad had undiagnosed depression. Don't get me started. Everyone's got a burden to bear.

I try never to forget there are people in situations worse than mine, much worse. But it wasn't until I was seventeen and had my accident and for a while saw myself as one of the unlucky ones—other people saw me that way, too, and some still do—that I stopped to appreciate how badly so many others have it, all the time, every day. Before then, the idea was pretty abstract. Then it became real, something I could feel for myself. After I had lived with my situation for a while, I realized: just because something really bad happened to me and made my life worse, suddenly and arbitrarily, didn't mean that the bad lot of other people had changed. Did I think, *Well, now there are fewer people in the world worse off than I am?* No, though I guess you could say that with that one incident in my life, a lot of people now "moved past" me on the luck-in-life scale.

My accident awakened and heightened my empathy for the world around me. I understood hardship better. I understood people better. For years now at Thanksgiving, we always invite a few people who, for one reason or another, don't have somewhere to go. In the end, as for how I felt about my fellow humans and what I was willing to do for them, my accident was a net gain. For certain others. And definitely for me.

And really, when you pit the possibilities against each other—having an unscarred face versus having a deeper appreciation for your fellow person, a deeper appreciation for being alive, and a greater sense of purpose about what to do with the life you've been blessed to live—is it even a contest?

Calamity puts things in perspective. Or it should, especially when it touches you directly, when it happens to someone you love or to you. It's not just a story you read about in the paper or hear someone recount about their friend's friend. I feel for people who feel terrible when trivial things go wrong and act as if they're not trivial. You can find those people across every socioeconomic level.

For my kids, my history helped to give them perspective, whether they liked it or not, especially when they were teens. When they were busy with typical high school-age activities—getting a driver's license, writing term papers and studying for exams, saving up for a car, going to the prom—they knew, if they stopped to think about it, that at approximately their age I was lying in a burn unit, intubated, desperate not to fall asleep because I didn't believe I would ever wake up. Or fighting to survive an infection that killed every patient in the ICU but me. Or just beginning my journey of dealing with massive, permanent scarring by undergoing the first of what would be dozens of surgeries. A bunch of crap I had no choice but to deal with. It became an unavoidable part of their family history. It forced me to grow up faster; a generation later, the memory and perspective of that forced Brian Jr., Matt, and Katie to grow up a little faster, too, or at least grow up with more-than-average compassion and thoughtfulness.

I didn't want to be reminding them at every turn of "what *I* went through at your age"—though I wasn't above alluding to it, if I felt they were getting a little too stressed about something that was, in the end, pretty trivial. ("You're worried about the social studies essay? Write it. If it sucks, it sucks. It's not like, you know, you might *die*....") One of the blessings in all this was that when my kids were going through high school and college, it was easy for them to confide in me with their worries and problems, because one's perspective at that age *can* get warped, and they knew I could bring them back to some sense of balance.

Here's another gift I gave my kids: because of the way I look, physical beauty is not one of the very top values they seek in a mate, as it is for many people (though Brian's wife Lisa happens to be very pretty). My kids grew up looking into my eyes, and loving this face solely because it belonged to their dad. That was the standard—the honesty of the eyes, my actions, my thoughts. Case closed. As Katie once said, "I didn't wake up one day as a kid or teenager and suddenly think, 'Wow! My dad looks different from everybody else!' He's my father. That's what he looks like. Actually, I would never say, 'That's what he looks like.' I just never think about it."

(Once, when Brian Jr. was very young, he asked me if I thought he would look like me when he grew up.)

What I look like gave them, in a way, a lot more room to choose, a lot of types to be attracted to. Katie says that whoever she's dating, she has never really cared about what the person could offer her in any other way but what was in their heart.

I know it's not just words with them. When Katie was ten, her hair started falling out. A total and very upsetting mystery, of course. She had no other obvious symptoms. Mary Ann and I and the doctors we visited during that difficult time had no idea the cause. Katie underwent all kinds of tests. During that episode, she stopped playing travel soccer for a month or two—but other than that interruption, she was surprisingly unfazed by the cosmetic upset. She didn't beg or even ask to stay home from school. Nothing. To be honest, she was almost disarmingly okay with it. You would think having your hair fall out, as a ten-year-old girl, would mess you up. But it didn't. She said she didn't care about her looks and it seemed to Mary Ann and me that she really meant it. Here's how she described it years later: "Okay, I don't have hair, I'm at an awkward stage of my life anyway, where I'm starting to mature…what difference does the hair make? Especially if I wasn't feeling sick and there were no other symptoms?"

Might this whole episode have played out differently if she had had another dad? I don't know. But she honestly didn't seem to mind walking around half-bald. (Ultimately, we discovered that it was alopecia caused by a nut allergy that she eventually outgrew.)

It's not just that my kids have the example of what I look like to view others, including possible mates. Maybe more important is that they had as an example a mother who fell in love with and married a guy whose face she hadn't even really seen for the first few months of their dating life, so she was really only going on the man's personality and mind and ability to make her laugh and feel confident, secure, respected, and happy. My kids have pointed out that those of their generation—also true of previous generations, I'll add here, so we don't seem to be singling out millennials—probably put a higher premium on looks than they do.

"For me," Brian Jr. once said, with incredible simplicity, "you have to be a good person first."

* * *

Years later, Mary Ann would insist that she couldn't remember the first time she saw me without the mask. It's not quite true to say she didn't know what I looked like when she first accepted my invitation to lunch. She *had* seen me—just not in person. As the assistant to the attorney handling my workers comp case, she had seen photographs of my face in the days following the fire—photos taken at St. Agnes to show the extent of the damage, pre- and post-initial skin grafts. A strong stomach helps.

So, yes, she had seen images of me. Yet somehow, she still managed to find me "attractive."

In the end, her feelings for me developed over many hours of phone conversations and meals and nights out, and that bond was strong enough that my disfigured face was a non-issue.

"It really didn't matter to me," she said.

How many people can manage *that* feat?

* * *

Bad as the pain was, it could have been worse.

The pain from getting burned was horrendous. But the pain from the wound-cleaning was worse.

Having my eyelids burned off was horrendous. But the pain from the corneal ulcers was worse.

My pain was horrendous. But the pain experienced by Milton and by the woman who was burned across 100 percent of her body and who lost her son and, ultimately, her own life from the car accident on the Schuylkill—that was much, much worse.

When I was intubated, I could not express in a raw way the pain I was feeling. (Writing down *I am in great pain* wouldn't have quite captured it.) But eventually the tube was removed and I could express it better. And the pain lessened and lessened and eventually went away.

There are so many people who can't adequately express their pain, so many who feel tremendous pain, so much of the time. If that fact about the rest of humanity doesn't make me grateful for all the good fortune and relatively painless days I have enjoyed in my life—even me, with my fire-disfigured face, and the reaction it sometimes engenders in people—well, that's on me.

* * *

Life is about having purpose and dignity. There. That's pretty much it. If you can help one person, then you have a purpose, and by helping

them gain dignity, you do, too. Problem solved, for both attributes,
both people.

Because when you help someone else, you help yourself in a way that
can't really be equaled by any other activity.

But nice as it may be, buying a homeless person whatever meal I'm
getting for myself or picking up a few Starbucks gift cards for them isn't
close to enough. I have to find a way to empower them to help themselves. That's the puzzle. That's the goal. When I joined the Million
Dollar Round Table Foundation, I felt as if I had discovered a charity
and an organization that looked at the world very much like I did, and
whose membership devoted its energies to doing what I enjoyed doing,
on a larger scale. Its values reminded me of those espoused in one of my
favorite movies, *Cinderella Man*, in which Russell Crowe plays the boxer
James J. Braddock, who fought during the Depression. Once he starts
making good money from his fighting, Braddock goes to the government office where he'd been receiving unemployment insurance to keep
his family afloat. He says, "I needed your help, I don't need it anymore,
here's your money back."

Aren't those some of the best parts of the American Dream—compassion and support, initiative and integrity—all in one?

I'm not meaning to make myself sound like the world's most selfless
person—far from it. I have a long, long way to go. And as emotive and
expressive as I became after my accident, I still often keep things in, even
as I know it helps no one (and may hurt me, most of all). I'll swallow
my stresses before I share them all with Mary Ann, my number one
foxhole person. I might open up to her about a troubling meeting or an
overbooked week, but I won't share my very biggest concerns, stuff that
weighs on me.

It was for this reason that I started to think about "seeing someone,"
talking about things I couldn't yet talk about with Mary Ann. Or anyone.

Just *thinking* about it, though. I had done it, briefly, years before,
very briefly.

And one thing I know for sure: what I have learned about people,
their pain, their hopes, their needs, all of it, made me not just a better

153

human being but also a much better businessperson. I hope that doesn't sound mercenary—I don't mean it like that. You know the old saying, "I went to a fight—and a hockey game broke out"? Well, I simply tried to live a good life—and a prosperous career broke out.

It can always be worse. I can often revert to imagining the worse-case (if not worst-case) scenario.

In reality, the best-case scenario happens, too.

CHAPTER 12:

Instead of Outrunning the Truth, Run with It

I don't want to die without any scars.
—Chuck Palahniuk, *Fight Club*

About a decade ago I got backed into seeing a therapist. My daughter was being bullied at her school. A girl Katie knew was getting bullied by lots of the "cool" girls, so Katie, my Katie, told them to back off, then started sitting every day at lunch with the girl, gradually becoming friendlier with her. The cool girls started bullying Katie, too.

Things got bad enough that I went to see the principal, a former nun. I was not interested to have her dissect the nuances of the situation to me. I simply told her, "Just so you know, I don't want a phone call down the line about this. I told Katie that if they do it to her one more time, just punch them right in the goddamn mouth."

"If that happens," the principal said, "I didn't see or hear anything."

I was stunned by her answer. Delighted. I couldn't help but think of the time that Johnny Glasson and Jack at The Irishman's claimed to the cop that they had witnessed nothing of Johnny's actions against the guy who had quietly ridiculed me at the bar.

"Thank you," I told the principal.

The one thing the principal insisted on was that Katie, Mary Ann, and I see a therapist—for general support, possible psychological and logistical strategies, and a compassionate ear, not as punishment for Katie. Given the principal's hands-off response to my threat, I figured I had to give her that one.

After the meeting with the principal, I gave Katie the update. "One more outburst from them, punch them right in the mouth. You have a green light. There will be no consequences, from me or the school. As a matter of fact, if you *don't* do it, I'll be pissed."

Toward the end of the first session the three of us had with the therapist, a very nice woman named Patty, she said she wanted to see Mary Ann and me for another session, just us. We did, and there I confessed to the therapist, "Yeah, I told Katie to beat the kids up."

The therapist took it in. She didn't say, "Are you a moron?" though she would have been within her right to do so. I'm sure it sounded like some pent-up anger at work. At the end of the session, she asked if it would be helpful for each of us alone to see her. I figured I owed her one, too, so I didn't push back. Also, I didn't want to make any more waves around Katie's situation.

But maybe I agreed so easily because something else was pulling at me.

When I showed up at the therapist's office for my solo, I was wary from the start, mostly because of my experience with mental health professionals (also, social workers and nuns) back in the burn unit. I would never discourage anyone from going to therapy of any sort if there was a chance it could help. But it wasn't my cup of tea. A few seconds after I sat down, the therapist said, "Can I ask what happened to you?"

"Sure," I said. I told her the story of my face.

When I was finished, she said, "How long were you in therapy?"

"I wasn't."

"What do you mean, 'I wasn't'?"

"It was offered. I didn't do it. I didn't have a good experience with the people doing it at the burn center, so I didn't do it when I got out, either."

She stared at me. "There's no way you could be this well-adjusted."

It was a compliment, though it sounded more than a little disbelieving. "Well, I am," I said, "and I didn't."

I saw her a couple more times by myself. I talked some more about the accident. I found it helpful—not to the degree that it changed my life, but I probably did have some coiled anger in me. Looking back, I probably should have seen someone sooner. Maybe it would have been an act of compassion, not indulgence or weakness, to put myself first, at least a little bit, by going to someone and talking about myself. I couldn't expect simply to outrun what I had been through, no matter how "well-adjusted" I seemed. No one can.

Fortunately for everyone, the bullying at Katie's school stopped. She didn't end up punching anyone. She had nothing to do with the cool girls, or they with her, and we were all fine with that.

* * *

Ours is a very close family. Those are the six best, most important words I will write in this book. I am certain that the closeness and love are reinforced by our openness with one another, a willingness to say what needs to be said—not meanly, but honestly, constructively. When I don't like you, you know it. When I love you, you know it.

I'm not opposed to occasional sarcasm to get my point across—but it's just honesty slightly couched in humor. Recently, Matt called after a period of no contact.

"Hey, Matt, what are you doing?" I asked.

"I haven't heard from you," he said.

"Yeah, I know."

"I haven't talked to you in, like, forever."

"It's been a week and a half."

"Is everything all right?"

"Everything is fine."

There was a pause.

"Well, I'll tell you," I said, "the phone works both ways. And I'm glad you called."

"Alright," he said. "I got you."

Humor is a great lubricant for criticizing loved ones. Or just because you want to rib them and it happens to be a very serious subject. Eight years ago, a couple months after Brian was in an awful car accident—a drunk driver going the wrong way on the highway—he was still in a lot of pain; it would be several more months before he could walk without limping. He was sitting on the couch watching a football game, his leg up. I stood over him. "You're *still* not over this?" I said. "It's been long enough."

He looked up at me and smiled. "Fuck you," he said. I smiled. I knew it was okay to rib him like that since he knew what I'd been through.

When the kids were much younger, Mary Ann came up with a brilliant idea called Open Mic Night. We do it to this day, though far less frequently; it doesn't seem as needed, and it's just rarer for us all to be together, especially with Matt in LA.

What's Open Mic Night? Every so often, usually after dinner, we gather in the living room and, one by one, each of us has to stand up and say something he or she wants to get off their chest. You can say whatever you want. You can vent. There are no repercussions. It's confession without a priest, revelation free of punishment. For me it's further proof that opening up brings people closer. The parents like it because it keeps everyone communicating on some meaningful level. The kids like it because, as they get older, it gets tougher for a parent to overreact. And keeping things in, even small things, does no one any good. Matt once used his Open Mic time to reveal something that he and Brian Jr. knew but Mary Ann and I didn't—that a few years earlier, Brian had friends over to the house one night, Matt came home, got pissed at something, he and Brian got into a fight, Matt threw a bottle of ketchup at Brian, and instead of the bottle hitting him it splattered all over the wall and the living room. All the boys helped clean the mess. Since Mary Ann and I had never noticed, I'm not sure why Matt felt the need to share this except to relieve him, and maybe Brian Jr., of their guilt. Honestly, my takeaway was that the boys and their friends were mature about handling a situation of their own making.

It became a family tradition, a healthy one, and over time it was the kids who would say, "We gotta have Open Mic Night."

Sometimes you were eager to have Open Mic Night, other times not so much. It really only worked when everyone participated, though there was no guarantee that each person's confession would be on the same scale. But each occasion was meant to open things up, bring us closer (in the end). Some nights were better than others. Some revelations seemed more important than others. No one ever confessed to killing anyone. Or hating anyone. No one ever said anything that made us profoundly have to rethink who they were.

Maybe Open Mic Night will work for you and your family or your circle. I can confirm that it does *not* work for everyone. Friends who heard about our tradition started their own night, and let's just say you've got to be careful with it. One of the kids in the family used Open Mic Night to lobby for a laptop computer, the mom got worked up in response, tears were shed by several parties, and the evening deteriorated from there. When we heard about the fiasco, we felt awful. I told the mom, "That's not how Open Mic Night works. If you're going to do that, just stop having them."

* * *

When Matt came out, he told me first. It's not that he preferred that to telling Mary Ann first, or both of us at the same time. It was merely circumstance.

I was down in South Carolina for a car show. Matt is the only one of my children who shares my weakness, at least a bit, for cars, and I thought it would be great if he came down to join me. When I picked him up at the airport, he seemed fidgety, not himself. I asked him what was wrong. Nothing, he claimed.

Given that I grew up in a very Catholic family—as did Matt—he may have thought I would flip out when I heard his announcement. Not that I had ever expressed homophobia or anything like it. He might have feared that it would change things between us—and since things were really good between us (I thought, and hoped he thought), such a change couldn't be viewed as a positive.

That first night in South Carolina, at dinner at our favorite restaurant, his discomfort continued.

"Matt, what's wrong?" I asked.

He shrugged, in pain.

"Nothing's that bad that you can't tell me," I said. "You can tell me anything."

After a very long pause, he said, "Dad, I'm gay."

I'm sure there was a long pause from me. It's not a moment I can ever re-do. I just hope the delay in my reaction wasn't more than a few seconds. If it was, I regret it.

In fact, my initial reaction was very calm. But when I'm unsure of something or get a little bit fearful—when I don't really know what to do, and there's no obvious plan, and the first responder in me can't just snap into action—I tend to get angry. Matt had once helpfully pointed out to me that anger and fear are two expressions of the same emotion. Now, while I was processing, Matt was thinking (he would say later), *Okay, Dad's going to get scared, then say something out of anger, which is really fear.* He was just waiting for it.

"Matt, I don't care, we don't care," I said, putting my arm around my son after I found my bearings. I had no idea. "I love you, we love you, no matter what," I said. We held each other's gaze. "Now let's decide what we're going to have for dinner."

I think of **the absolute most important lessons I learned after my accident:**

Look in the mirror. Know yourself. Be yourself.

Live your life the way you want, never mind what anyone else may think, because it's your life. Trust your judgment.

Trust that those around you get you and love you.

They all applied perfectly to Matt in this case. They apply to him and everyone in all cases.

Matt's news didn't change anything. I don't mean to make that sound glib. But in the long run, it didn't change anything important.

* * *

The truth changes. A lot of what was true before the fire was not true after. The truth is changing all the time, for everyone, in big ways and small. Often you don't recognize the change has happened—but it has. **There's always a new normal.**

As a parent, the truth changes as your children get older and as you add children and then grandchildren to the family. The circumstances in which the kids grow up change, so their experiences are different from one another, no matter how close they are in age or temperament. The family living space may be different, the struggle for money may be different, the experience level of the parents is certainly different.

How children see their parents changes, of course. It happened for me. At the time of the accident, I appreciated that it was miserable for my mother and father to see me suffer. But I was focused on how hard it was for me.

As I got older, I saw things more deeply. (You would hope so.) I had my criticisms of my mother and sometimes lost patience with her, and still do. Over the years, though, if I needed something, she would come through, always. And I would remind myself of what she had gone through. Here's a woman who had four kids of her own. Then a horrible accident happened in her husband's family and suddenly she had three more children to care for. Then she got pregnant with her fifth child—though really her eighth—and he died in childbirth in April 1963, thirteen months before I arrived. The baby died within an hour of entering the world. No explanation was ever given. Maybe there wasn't one. Perhaps worst of all, my mother never got to see him. The doctor or nurse took the baby from the delivery room. The hospital called an undertaker, who came and took her child away.

Life didn't always turn out the way my mother thought it would, either.

The truth changed with my father. As I was growing up, he was not a patient or warm man. The first time my father ever told me "I love you" was the night of the fire, in the burn center, when it looked like I was going to die. Given his deep Catholicism, saying those words might have been more for him than for me. I loved my father immensely, but he could treat me brutally at times. Then again, he never treated me differently from any of my brothers or sisters, nor was Dad warmer to anyone outside the family. When Mary Ann and I had been dating a while, I would sometimes sleep at her house rather than drive back to mine, forty-five minutes away, or she might sleep at ours. In the latter case, if she took a morning shower deemed "too long" by Dad, he would go to the water valve, shut it off, and yell up, "That's it, you're done!" Once, in the hospital, I got upset about my situation; I can't remember the precise issue. "You gotta buck up!" Dad barked. "No crying! This is the hand you're dealt." He seemed to believe you could steamroll your problems or avoid acknowledging them altogether. Almost every day of my childhood, when he would come home from his unsatisfying jobs—first in sales for a company that sold church paraphernalia (chalices, missalettes, bibles, and such), then as personnel director for the company, then in personnel for other companies—he didn't talk about work. He didn't talk about much of anything. He would sit silently at the dinner table. If any of us had caused some trouble that day, it was addressed. If not, you weren't spoken to. Then he would retire to the bedroom he shared with my mother. And that's where he stayed, alone. There was no family game night, no Open Mic Night, almost never watching TV together. What he did in there all evening—read? Just lay on the bed?—I don't know. If you wanted to communicate with him, you did it through the door. Once, when I was thirteen, I needed ten dollars to go on a school field trip. After he came home from work and joined the family for a quick dinner in his sullen mood, he retreated as usual to the bedroom. I asked my mom about the money and she told me to ask my dad. I went and knocked on their bedroom door. "Yeah," came the gruff voice from inside.

"It's Brian," I said.

"What do you want?"

"I need money for a field trip tomorrow."

"How much?"

"Ten dollars."

There was no hesitation on his end. "We don't have ten dollars." No explanation, either.

There was a brief pause on my end. "Oh, okay," I said.

It's hard to have a debate with someone who has put up a barrier and can't be seen. The next day, forty-four of the forty-five kids in my grade went on the field trip. I sat in a classroom alone. All I had was a book, and reading was not my favorite activity.

Maybe my father was a loner. More likely, he was lonely. Looking back, I think he suffered from depression, though they rarely gave people medication to manage it back then. He could be sarcastic, brusque. He was twelve when he lost his father. He lost a brother and sister-in-law to a tragic car accident, then accepted the responsibility of looking after three of his nieces and nephews. Two years before my accident, my older brother Ed was stabbed in a fight behind a bar and almost died. I'm sure all that took something out of Dad, as did what happened to me. Dad was the one who called the other kids that night to tell them, *Brian's been hurt, come to the hospital, right away, Brian may not make it through the night.* He never talked to me about what that did to him. For a long time, I didn't have the life perspective to understand just how much it must have taken from him.

The last ten, twenty years of my father's life? Totally different. He softened. Some of it was the effect I think I had on him, because of the effect that Mary Ann's more openly loving, expressive family had on me. I wanted to give my father the time and experiences with my children that he hadn't been able to enjoy with his own, emotionally and financially. Eventually, amazingly, my dad became a hugger. For a while there, it was surreal for me that my kids saw my father only in a very kindly light. When they would hear me tell stories about growing up, and Dad's orneriness and temper, they didn't believe me. "That's not true about Pops," they insisted. "No way."

"It's absolutely true," I told them. But I'm their father, so they didn't completely buy it. "Renee," I'd say, when my sister was with us, "am I telling the truth?"

"Absolutely," she would confirm, then turn to my kids. "Your grandfather was a different man then."

The lesson I learned from all this is not that things change, especially with the passage of a great many years. It's that you must *recognize that change has happened, or is happening, and then change your attitudes accordingly.*

It doesn't take a genius to recognize when a truth has changed suddenly, like when someone's face has nearly burned off in the course of a few minutes. It takes real skill to appreciate that things have changed slowly, things that seemed as if they would never or could never change. When my father died, of course it was incredibly tough. But I made myself remember that, for all the difficulties over so many years, he had been brought into the womb of love of our family, and love was something he had trouble expressing as I was growing up (and also back when he was a kid growing up). I made myself remember a trip we all took to Ireland, our ethnic homeland, where he had never been before, and that moment when he was standing there as part of a foursome with Matt, Brian Jr., and me, at the first tee at Portmarnock. My father turned to me and hugged me and said, "I love you. Thank you."

* * *

You can change the truth, you can make a new story—though it really helps first to have something better with which to replace the old truth, the tired story. There was the time, years ago, when my great friend and business partner Kevin told me he was getting married the coming November. I was honored that he wanted me in his wedding party. But then a snafu in plans meant they had to change the wedding date to October 24th.

Except for Mary Ann and our kids, I never let anyone in on what I did every October 24th, the anniversary of the fire. I never called attention to it the way you might a birthday (if your family and friends were to accidentally overlook it). Each time the date rolled around, I simply did not show up at the office. I didn't say anything to Kevin or to my assistant on that date. They would assume I was in the field that day, meeting clients. No one had reason to think otherwise. I would spend it alone. Not hanging around the house. Somewhere out, but alone.

When Kevin told me innocently about his new wedding date, I couldn't hide my look of trepidation.

"What is it?" he asked, concerned.

I told him it was the anniversary of the accident.

"Jesus Christ," said Kevin. "I didn't know. I'm so sorry—"

"No," I said, "this is really cool. It gives me a chance now to look forward to the date instead of dreading it."

The morning of that October 24th, mine was the first car in the church parking lot, before anyone else from the bridal party. I always show up early to commitments, but in this case, I probably overdid it. Of course, I was there, first and foremost, to respect the specialness of the day for Sandie and Kevin. But I was also there to prove to myself that this day could be imbued with a different meaning, once and for all.

CHAPTER 13:

Embrace the Unknowable

The best preparation for the future is to live as if there were none.
—Albert Einstein

Prior to my accident, my faith was tenuous, at best. When I found myself lying in a bed in an ICU burn unit, I had trouble believing that Jesus had been up there thinking about me and just decided sometime in my senior year of high school to throw me into a fire.

As you might imagine, my thoughts were spinning in the months after. Occasionally I would let my guard down. "I don't understand why God did this to me," I once said to my good friend Mike Smith. "I'm fucking seventeen. What did I do to deserve this?"

"Brian, I don't really know what to tell you," said Mike. He was seventeen, too. I respected his helplessness. I don't know that age would have made a difference.

The unknowable lives in us every day. For me, burned lungs are an issue, decades after the accident. The remnants from the fire have never fully gone away. I just had my yearly physical and the chest x-ray showed what appear to be crystals sitting at the bottom of my lungs. The building I was in that night was probably built in the 1950s, which means it may well have had asbestos. I don't know for sure. But you can make a good guess. Either way, whatever's sitting in my lungs, along with scarring, has reduced my capacity over the years. I get shortness of breath sooner than I should. I hope that's the worst of it.

* * *

Every time you enter a burning building, something big and terrible can happen to you. Something really big and good can be taken from you. Permanently. But that's a secondary consideration. Your primary consideration is to do everything you can to keep bad, permanent things from happening to strangers who desperately need your help.

If nothing bad had happened to me that night, I would still be grateful and respectful for the life I had. I'm sure of it. The experience of fighting fires and dealing regularly with life-and-death situations does that to a person.

But something *did* happen that night, one of the worst things that can happen to a firefighter short of dying, and my gratitude and respect for life went to another level. Because the reality of what happened to me brought home that thing we all keep telling ourselves but rarely live as if it's true: you *don't* know when it will happen.

It is this that makes me try to listen to everyone extra carefully, to really hear what they're saying. Makes me try to engage deeply. (The smartphone is slowly killing that ability for everyone, even as some of us fight it.) When I look back someday, way in the future, if I'm lucky to get that far and I still have my wits, I want to remember that *I was there*. That I lived deeply. That I wasn't half-listening or distracted. That I heard. That I was making eye contact. That I was present in my life. The only person who can be present or not in my life is me.

Life is a gift, not a given.

* * *

Pro tip: don't have too many family members die within a ninety-day period.

My two dads—my father Ed and my father-in-law Jim—died within eight weeks of each other in the spring of 2018. Johnny Glasson died a week after my father. My mother-in-law Millie died a little more than a month after that. Mary Ann and I and the kids did not have enough time between the deaths to process each person's passing. In a way, we had to grieve for all of them simultaneously. It wasn't really fair to the memory of each person.

But I remember some things vividly. There is an odd, intense peacefulness (can peacefulness be intense?) to looking into the eyes of someone right before they die. For both my father and my father-in-law, I was one of those looking in their eyes in those final moments.

I think it was peaceful for them, too. Or I want to believe that. I need to believe that. And maybe "peaceful" is not the right word. It was a gift, a poignant moment with each of them I'll cherish the remainder of my life—knowing I did it for them but that I got at least as much out of it. Knowing that something so deep—gratitude? love?—passed between us. I don't know.

Those final days, and especially those final moments, take their toll on you, emotionally and psychologically. But I would not give up the experience of being there for anything, draining as it is. Twice, I've had to put dogs of ours down, Lila and Brady, and I was staring at them when it happened. I absolutely bawled my eyes out. After the second one, Brady, I told Mary Ann and the kids, "I'm not doing this again." A day or two after Millie died, I told Mary Ann, "Thank god we're almost out of parents. I'm not going through that again."

Rodger the Undertaker is a close friend, an incredibly decent man and a true professional, but I was damn tired of giving him business. I asked him how many funerals he did a year. "About one hundred," he said. Having our family provide three percent of his annual revenue for 2018 was more than enough.

At the luncheon following my father's memorial service, my cousin Marjorie, Uncle Dick's daughter, approached me. We hardly knew each other, but she had stayed in touch with my parents over the years, just as I had with her dad who had died five years earlier.

"Brian, I'm so sorry for your loss," she said. "Your dad was a great guy." She asked about his final days. I told her that many of us sat with him, and I felt it was a privilege to spend so much time with him at the very end.

"I remember my father's last days," she said. "He did the craziest thing. We were all sitting around his bed and he started making these motions with his hands, and one of us asked him if everything was okay, and he said, 'Fine, I'm fishing with Ed and Bill.'"

"What?" I said.

My friend Tommy Glasson was listening in on the conversation and told me later that I turned white as a ghost. Once, during my father's last days, I noticed his left hand was closed and still while his right hand was moving in a small circular motion. It wasn't palsy. There was something very intentional going on and I asked him what he was doing. "Fishing," he said. Growing up, I had never fished with my father. Not once. "I'm fishing with Dick and Bill," he said, referring to his brothers.

"We don't remember Dad ever fishing," continued Marjorie, "but he said he was fishing with his brothers. I guess they fished together as boys."

I regained some composure and told Marjorie that my father had done the same thing.

What we understand now is so tiny compared to what we have yet to understand.

* * *

We don't get to decide how long people will be in our lives.

With all the dying going on in my life, it was natural to think about what would no longer be. But I also had to think positively about what *was* that didn't have to be. *I* didn't have to be here. I could easily not have been. I was grateful for everyone who was still in my life and had been for so many years.

I thought of a moment from several years ago. Brian Jr. was still recovering from his car accident, and I was helping my nephew Ed Jr. move out of the apartment that he and Brian Jr. had shared. The place was across the street from a church, and while we were moving the boys' stuff out, there was a funeral procession. Mourners headed into the church as bagpipes played. Maybe it was the sound of the bagpipes that stopped me—they get to almost everyone, I assume, but especially if you're Irish—and I said to Ed Jr., "If things had gone just a little differently with Brian's accident, that could have been all of us over there."

"Oh, come on," said Ed Jr.

He thought I was being melodramatic. He wasn't yet a father.

* * *

I believe some things are meant to be. There's a reason people come in and out of your life. The people in your life are meant to be in your life when they're there. However long they stay in your life, that's meant to be, too. I don't claim to know the reason why them, why then, why for however long they stay. And why you stay in *their* life. Whether they're there for a ten-minute encounter or the rest of your life, though, there's a reason.

And the reason is…you make the reason. Or not.

I don't believe my getting caught in that fire was "meant to be," as if I was chosen. If that's true, then I should believe that every person ever caught in a fire or killed in a fire was meant to have that happen, and everyone who wasn't was also meant to happen. And everyone who experiences calamity was meant to go through it, and everyone who avoided it was similarly destined for that set of circumstances. I don't believe that at all. I do believe that, at least for me, I was presented with an opportunity—destined or random, doesn't matter. It was a moment that could define me, or that I could define. I do not think I was picked. I do think I had a choice.

You can't really face the unknowable, by definition. Can there be any lessons then? Sure. ***Moments happen, no matter what you think you're going to do to stop them from happening. But either the moments define you or you define the moments.***

That's one lesson.

CHAPTER 14:

Face Yourself (If You Think You Have, You Still Probably Haven't)

We have two lives…the life we learn with and the life we live after that.
—Bernard Malamud

To this day, I would like to kill the firefighter who abandoned me. He went out a nearby window and found the tall ladder. You think he could have maybe given me a heads-up?

I saw him three months after the fire, at the annual banquet installing new members into the fire company. He was not from the Levittown company but Edgely. He approached me. I guess that's a form of bravery.

"I want to talk to you about what happened back there," he said. Nice euphemism, *back there.*

"Really, is there anything to say?" I replied.

"I apologize for leaving you."

He was looking for absolution. I was not interested in granting it, not that it was ever mine to give.

"Okay," I said flatly, not giving him the satisfaction. "You're trained to never do that. And you did. This is the consequence of that." Another doozy of a euphemism, *this*.

Johnny Glasson, one of my rescuers and a firefighter's firefighter, was seated at my table. He overheard everything.

"Holy shit!" he said to me after the fellow finally walked away, unabsolved.

Confrontation is at the heart of my story. So many of us avoid it at all costs. And make no mistake: ***There is always a cost to avoiding confrontation, especially if the one you're avoiding is you.***

* * *

Maybe I don't know myself as much as I think.

Not that long ago, I was talking with Brian Jr. and a few of his friends and the subject of expectations came up. One friend asked Brian if he measured himself against me. Brian said, "It's not as easy as people think."

Not the answer I was prepared for. "What does that mean?" I asked.

"You have pretty high standards," said Brian. "They're not so easy to live up to."

Were we talking about the same person? "I never put standards on anybody," I said. "I never told you what to do for a living, or you had to do well in school, never even told you you had to go to college. I never told you one thing you *had* to do."

"You didn't have to," he said.

I was floored. I had no idea. In my mind, I was the anti-helicopter parent. I was there whenever my kids needed me, particularly for the major moments, but did not involve myself in the littler things. I did not try to influence them in ways I felt I shouldn't; we need to discover our passions ourselves. I tried my best to strike a balance: When Brian, a standout golfer in high school—a two handicap—wondered out loud about pursuing a professional golf career, I told him, "I'm your dad, and I'll support your pursuing whatever you want. But just know that you're going to have to give it everything you have—and even then, it's a very,

very long shot." Later on, I was thrilled when Brian became a police offi-cer (before he changed careers and went into finance) because it meant that if I'd given off even a little vibe that I wished he would become a fireman, he had seen beyond that to his own place, his own way to do public service. At his graduation from the academy, I told him how proud I was.

Obviously, I had also made an impression over the years that I didn't think I was making. It didn't particularly hurt me, but it did surprise me.

Not too long ago, my mother-in-law was advising Katie to get out more, the way that, years ago, she had advised her daughter, my future wife, to get out more (and to dump that loser, Chuck, though she didn't have to actually say that to Mary Ann). "Katie, there are lots of people out there to date," said Millie.

"The problem," said Katie, "is I'm trying to find somebody like my dad."

Again, I thought I was hearing wrong. "Like *what*?" I said. "Why? Your mother will tell you, I'm no peaches and cream."

"Dad, I like good food, I like good wine, and twenty-five-year old guys generally don't care much about that," she said. "I also want some-one with a good heart who makes me laugh. I'm not going to settle."

"I'm not telling you what to do, but I think you might want to bring down your expectations. Your mother fell in love with an eighteen-year-old burn victim. And her parents probably thought I was creepy. At first, anyway."

Because I had to confront myself at age seventeen, like it or not, and because I chose a path of self-starting and straight-shooting and no bull-shitting, I assumed that for all my adult life, I knew exactly who I was and the impression I was making on those around me. That's not to say I thought that everyone liked me; I was certain many people *didn't*. But at least I could read them, or so I thought. I didn't need to talk to some professional to discover who I really was. I was fine, mentally strong. When anyone in my big circle needed me, they knew they could count on me. Just pick up the phone. I was the foxhole person for so many people in my life. I loved that. I was reliable, predictable, an easy book to read. I didn't wear a mask.

I knew who I was.

Really?

* * *

In the months after my accident, I kept thinking, *I'm going to look like I did before.* I wasn't ready to let go of that delusion. I couldn't, not yet. It took me a long, long time to accept the reality. Eventually I did. Had I never accepted it, I would have become a bitter jerkoff. Who knows if I would have accomplished anything for others? Probably not, since I wouldn't have cared about it, or me, or them. Who knows if I would have cared even to still be around?

Did the events of October 24, 1981, cheat me out of certain experiences? Absolutely. In a way, I stopped growing up that day. That night I simply became a grownup, like it or not. I missed a lot of the experiences my friends went through. All those people had a really good time (not every second of every day—but come on) while I was going through crap. I would like to have been "normal." I would like to know what the last almost forty years would have been like, normal. Just being drowned out in the crowd, not being stared at in every mall or hotel lobby. Sitting at a bar or in a restaurant without feeling someone's eyes.

That's not my reality, though. For the person in the wheelchair, for the blind, the deaf, the very short, the very tall, the very fat: that's not their physical reality. We're all over the place, and we can't hide. Maybe we don't have it worse than everyone else, those who are hiding in plain sight. But the one advantage "regular people" have—and sometimes it might be no advantage at all, or even a disadvantage—is that their "condition" isn't immediately obvious.

Acceptance. Until you forgive for the wrong that was done you, genuinely forgive all who were concerned—one person, many people, God, the cosmos, someone or something with no name, whoever or whatever, yourself?—you carry that grudge or meanness inside you. It comes out in one form or another. The bitterness that festers from not accepting what happened has ruined countless lives, both the person wronged and, often just as bad, many of those around that person. You can be bitter about people dying too soon, or even just dying period, or dying one after the other in a very short time span. You can be bitter about an opportunity that should have gone to you but, for a bunch of unfortunate factors or maybe just dumb bad luck, did not. You can be bitter about a terrible accident that happened, mangling your face forever.

Until you accept the reality, though, you can't go on, not really. In truth*, there are only two choices before you at all times.*

1. Accept what happened.

2. Slowly be ruined by what happened.

I'm not saying acceptance and forgiveness are easy. I understand it might be easier for some, armed with a certain personality or outlook. On some level, though, we all have to accept our circumstances, the ones we can't change. We can't expect to eliminate or diminish the negative effects of the reality until we accept it.

I thought that I had accepted what happened to me. True, some moments still got to me. It was always tough for Johnny Glasson and me to be together. I was invited every year to a picnic for local firefighters, many of whom I knew. Year after year I declined the invitation because it was more than an hour from home, and family plans always seemed to get in the way. Maybe I purposely let them get in the way, then told myself a plausible story. One year I finally told Mary Ann, "Okay, I'll go and bring the kids, too." Brian Jr. was twelve at the time. He had met Johnny before, but he may have been too young to know what he wanted to say or didn't yet have something to say. Now, when we arrived at the picnic, I introduced my children to all the guys. When Brian was re-introduced to Johnny, he looked him up and down, as if confirming he was real this time, then reached out his hand to shake. "Thank you," said little Brian, "for saving my dad's life." Johnny started crying.

Yet I didn't. I focused my energy on my surprise at Brian Jr.'s maturity. I didn't react to the upshot of the exchange.

Not crying in that moment should have been a sign that I still had work to do.

* * *

I know I have made progress. They talk about "what was lost in the fire," but I can easily talk about what was gained, too. I would almost certainly not have met Mary Ann. If I had not met Mary Ann, we would not have these three particular, incredible children. I would not have the amazing daughter-in-law and granddaughter we have. Many blessings have come to me because of that event. Having a completely burned face gave me a kind of superhuman mental strength, the feeling that I could overcome anything. Being liberated to go my own way and being a self-starter, I don't have to be reverential to any individual or company or organization. The world didn't exactly go my way, at least not when I was seventeen and a half, so I can exploit that advantage, too. When I am polite (which I am, most of the time), it means something.

If not for the fire, life would have been different for me, very different. And because I love my life, it's hard to imagine how it could be better. Corny as it sounds, I can say that in some ways, the accident was the best thing that happened to me. I know it sounds sick. But if given the chance, I don't know that I would trade the experience.

And look at the mood I approach life with! I rarely feel despair—you know, down in the dumps, hopeless. How could I? I'm fortunate to have enjoyed some success in my field, and while I like to believe I might have been successful regardless (though maybe in a different field), I might well have lacked the perspective and empathy and especially the sense of urgency that my life circumstance gifted me. I think it's why I have always raced a hundred miles an hour. When I assess my life to this point, I look at how I did not let that moment at the Edgely Apartments or the aftermath define me. Instead I used the lessons I learned from all that to make me better than I was, better than I probably ever would have been. Lester Rosen would be proud. I found an inner strength, another gear, and not just because I was young. Positive, honest, sometimes brutal self-evaluation has helped me to accept what happened.

I'm even okay with how I look. Millie, my late mother-in-law, liked to say to Mary Ann, "I think he's handsome now, to tell you the truth." God bless you, Millie.

*   *   *

I've always tried to get Mary Ann to be less of a "what-if?" person. *What if this happens? What if that happens?* My response is always, "And what if it doesn't?" What-if can cast a shadow of fear over your life, I tell her. What-if can paralyze you. I'm a walking, talking canvas for what-if thinking: When strangers look at me, they're not seeing me but asking themselves: *What if something that bad happened to me? What if something that bad hadn't happened to that guy?*

I try to banish the what-ifs.

But as I have become more honest with myself, I have to admit that Mary Ann is not the only one in the family who plays the what-if game.

I just don't say it out loud as much.

Look: it shouldn't have happened. Most fires shouldn't. Most disasters shouldn't. So many things have to go wrong for something big and terrible to happen. Then again, so many things have to go right for something big and beautiful to happen, right?

I should not have been up there. It was a crappy firewall. The wood paneling was cheap, though it made the apartments look handsomer. I happened to be on call. Had one of the many things that led to the spark turning into a flame turning into a fireball not happened, the Levittown and Edgely Fire Departments would have had a quiet evening. Or, if the fire had stayed small, Edgely would have responded, but we in Levittown would not have been second call. I would have slept until morning, after a night spent with the Murthas eating Burger King.

Had it all happened five years later, with me getting caught, maybe I don't heal as well. Maybe I don't have the resiliency I showed. Maybe I do.

There is randomness in every moment. A decision—the opportunity to make a decision—is the fork in the road where humans get to take just a little bit of the randomness out of the equation.

How can I not be glad about the choices I made? Especially when the rest of my life rests on the principle that action is good, inaction bad? Too many people don't fully acknowledge or maybe even understand that *not choosing is a choice.* I never want to just leave things alone, to let them "happen" without my positive influence. To stand on the sidelines. I want to stamp the moments, the situation, with my presence. To live the life I want to, I need to take responsibility by shaping it. Resignation, surrender, passivity—those are not good looks. And leaving things alone is not really leaving things alone. It's more negative than that. It's taking the attitude that things *probably* won't work out. Like, what's the point? If that's your attitude, probably you're going to get exactly what you think you will.

I like to think I've been a good dad, though my kids get to make the final call. I attended practically every youth sports event they were involved in growing up, coaching when I could. I was at every recital, show, and parent-teacher conference. I hope I did a good job given the particular demands of my work—long hours (often going until eight or nine in the evening, missing many family meals), considerable travel, and occasional unscheduled client emergencies. But because I want to do everything I can, and do it right, I have regrets. I am very close to my children, yet I wish I were closer. I wish I had listened to them more instead of rushing in, always the first responder, to try to solve their problems for them because I couldn't bear to see them suffer, because I thought my problem-solving abilities were so wonderful and immediately required. If I could trade some work success for a history of more sit-down dinners with them, I'd do it in a second—but even if I could magically make that happen, it wouldn't unfold exactly as I'm imagining, where you can peel back just a little, the drudgery part, and in turn make it up with the most fun family meals. To achieve a certain kind of professional success in a competitive field, you had better be all in or don't bother.

And what would I be feeling now if I *had* had much more limited professional success? Maybe I would be lamenting how I had not modeled a good work ethic for my kids. You can never totally win.

Regret is like a weed: it will find a way, no matter the circumstance.
I *do* have regrets in my life. A lot of stupid stuff has come out of my mouth that I wish hadn't. I've spent more money on cars than I care to admit.

I no longer regret what happened that October night at Edgely.

There it is. I guess all I'm saying is: never forget that in life, you don't get a do-over for a particular year or day or hour or minute. So if things don't go your way in that minute or hour or day or even year, be ready to do something about it.

* * *

What do people think of when they think of you? What will people say about you when you go? What do you want perpetuated beyond your death? Or are you one of those who truly don't care about that?

Whatever they say about me, I want to know what it is NOW. Not for the ego stroke (assuming there's something nice to say), but I want to know that I am doing enough while I can still make more of an effort; if it's not enough, speak up! Please tell me so I can fix it. *Now.*

I want my reputation to be an accurate reflection of what has mattered to me in my life. Where the result is almost as indistinguishable from what I had aimed for as the reflection in a mirror is to the person peering into it. If you're lucky, you think, *Yep, that's me.*

* * *

I have made real progress. And there's still a lot of work to do.

A year ago, out of the blue, I picked up the phone to call someone I hadn't talked to in ten years. I say "out of the blue" because I don't know why I was moved to do it right then.

No, that's not true. I know why. It's because of this. These words.

I called the therapist, Patty, that Katie, Mary Ann, and I had all seen back when Katie was being bullied in school. The therapist who had then seen me alone.

"I'd like to talk to you for half an hour," I told Patty over the phone. She agreed to find time.

After I entered her office and we exchanged pleasantries, she said, "I'm surprised to see you here."

I told her I was about to start writing a book about what my life had taught me, how my experience at seventeen had profoundly affected everything after. "I don't know if it might help to see you while I'm going through this writing experience," I said. "Maybe some of these memories will trigger something where I would want to see you. That's really the purpose of my visit."

Just being there and saying that was a good start, I guess. I would have to stand back a few feet from my somewhat old-fashioned, self-fashioned role in the family as the protector. I never shared real intimacies or, in Jim Noonan's word, "fears." I never felt comfortable burdening my wife or my kids with anything that was bothering me deeply. I would call up a friend now and then and say, "Hey, let's go grab a couple drinks and shoot the shit." But that was more about deflecting hard truths, not confronting them.

Patty and I talked about how everything has to come out, one way or the other, sooner or later. And it's a lot better if it's sooner. Suppression may be an aim for a firefighter—Levittown No. 2 specialized in search, rescue, and suppression—but it's a terrible strategy psychologically, individually. Suppressing feelings makes for greater anxiety or panic attacks or a darker worldview or the occasional blowup that seems to come from nowhere.

There is simply no hiding from yourself.

Funny thing is, for all my resistance to therapy, a lot of my own job the last quarter-century is very much like that. When you take care of somebody's finances, you're a part-time psychologist. You'd better be a great listener. You have to know which things they're saying are important and which aren't. Maybe I like my job because I get to listen, and I prefer to understand what's going on with other people than with myself.

But I do know myself. I do. I know what I love and like and hate. I love Mary Ann, my kids, my family, my friends. My favorite place in the world is Hilton Head, South Carolina, the only place where I experience true solitude and where I get more quality time with the kids in seven days than the whole rest of the year. I love the music of Frank Sinatra, Adele, classic rock. I love the TV show *Law & Order* (who doesn't?). I love the Three Stooges. I love *It's a Wonderful Life, Fletch, The Godfather.* On a flight to Italy, I almost got all three *Godfathers* in; I think the second one's actually superior to the the first, and the less said about the third, the better. I hate cheapness, status-climbers, people who always have an agenda. People who can't take a joke or even know when one is being made. I am comfortable in my skin, a lot more than many people I encounter. I feel for them, truly.

But when I go deeper, I admit it: there *are* moments when I still think I would give it all back to look like I did, or what I might have looked like now. Every now and then, a client visit or an errand will take me near Levittown and I'll make it a point to drive down my old street. The house, 14 Quaint Road, is in the middle of the block. The Jubilee. It was a mostly Irish and Italian Catholic neighborhood, but we had the Goldblooms on one side of us, the Mushnickis on the other, the Stoeckles across the street. A great mix of people. Mark Smith lived over in Juniper Hill, Tom Stewart in Upper Orchard. Different neighborhoods, different tracts of houses. I remember my sister Renee walking me to and from kindergarten, a tiny school attached to a church with a cemetery just before it that we had to pass on the way there and back. She was almost ten and I was five, and we used to make jokes, looking at the headstones and guessing at how this or that person died. Was it a car accident? Were they sick?

There was a creek down from our house where everyone would hang out, especially as we got older. We rode our bikes to each other's homes. We played in a hockey league where we rented ice time at four in the morning. Everyone seemed to be a decent athlete or a really good one. If the Glassons were around—and with thirteen of them, there were always Glassons around—you knew a fight could break out any minute, Glasson against someone or Glasson on Glasson. So many of the neighborhood families had men who were World War II veterans who, along with their wives, had put a hundred dollars down for their dream home, costing somewhere between five and ten thousand bucks in total, and started families. There were enough kids around for every one of my siblings to have at least one friend of the same age to hang out with, play stickball or rollerblade with. I can almost see myself there. That Brian is defined by many things, some good, some bad. None of them has to do with being caught in a fire. That Brian's face is notable only for its long lashes. His hair is parted in the middle. An all-around decent-looking kid.

There's an alternate universe where that Brian gets burned, just like the actual one did, but over the years, his fight to still see the world in a positive light is not going well. Like many people who struggle with negativity, he continually revisits the injustice of it, the slights that came from it, the people he's no longer on speaking terms with because of it, the most recent person who wronged him. There's always an enemy. There's always drama, and not the good kind. There's always collateral damage, with other relationships compromised. It's the era of Facebook, so this alternative Brian may have unfriended some people, or been unfriended himself. To be close with this Brian is hard work. His friends always feel as if they're walking on eggshells because they don't want to be next on his Enemies List. There's no nice way to put it. It's work.

Fortunately, that's not the world I live in. That's not the person I became. I know many people like that, and I try my best to help them. Now, I realize how difficult it is to help. Maybe that's a weird admission for someone writing a book with thoughts about how to live your best life. The most useful advice I can give anyone, including myself, is to control yourself, which is enough of a challenge. Once I make peace with the fact that I'm the only one I can control, I realize all the options I have to determine how positive or negative I can make my life. I have chosen the positive way, the active way, the decisive way.

I was smart enough to know that writing this book could dredge up some difficult thoughts.

*   *   *

Some things about my life are particular to my situation and some are not. Tonight and every night for the last thirty-seven years, I put ointment on the inside of my left eye and sometimes my right so that they don't dry out because my right eyelid closes only part way and my left eyelid not at all.

I get periodically "stretched out" and have ever since the accident. It's like massage therapy for my skin and muscles because of all the graft surgeries.

My lung capacity is compromised, but you might not know it if you saw me going hard in spinning class for forty-five minutes. Then again, when the trainer comes to the house to get me to work out, I mostly want to talk so I can avoid the cardio. When I golf, I usually walk the course, so you might not know that I had more than my share of scar tissue built up.

You can hardly tell that skin from my left thigh was used for my first facial graft; the "scarlet red"—gauze bathed in Betadine—used in the healing turned into a big scab, fell off, and it looks pretty good, painful as it was. When they took skin from my right thigh for the second graft, though, they experimented with a method that was supposed to be less painful, and it was—but it left a giant scar. I guess there's a metaphor in there.

Katie is doing a great job as an internal wholesaler at Lincoln Financial. They love her there. Everyone loves her. She's a funny one. Like me, she's stubborn and does what she wants, not what other people think she should do. (I like to say I share a name with Brian, a birthday—May 19—with Matt, and an attitude with Katie.) In high school she was an all-county soccer player—and then just grew tired of it. She wasn't enjoying it, so she quit, even as coaches and teammates encouraged her to reconsider. When she didn't, they all wondered why she did what she did. Why? Because she didn't like it anymore, that's why. The first and only time Katie played golf, she went bogey, bogey, par, bogey, off the men's tees. She had hit balls at the range before but never played a hole on a real golf course. When we walked off the fourth green, she turned to me and said, "I'm done."

"What?" I said.

"This is boring," she said. "I don't like it."

"You're beating both your brothers right now."

"I don't like it."

She never played again.

Matt will succeed at whatever he does and wherever he is. He's such a quick study. He's great at business but even better with people, generally. In his current job he has to handle the complaints of customers, especially the wealthy, which not everyone can do well (and not everyone would want to do well). His company is so lucky to have him.

He's our toughest kid. He's like me—not a hard read at all. If he doesn't like you, you know it. I love that he says whatever's on his mind, appropriate or not. I don't think he's found his professional or life passion just yet but whatever it turns out to be, he will make a mark.

Brian Jr. has been with our firm for just over two years now. He has the fire in his belly to be successful. He's got a very even-keeled personality, even unflappable—completely unlike me. But underneath he's got real drive and initiative. Recently I mentioned something about how a client I had just seen would need something—and the next time I brought up the client's name, Brian said, "I took care of it."

"Everything," I said, meaning it more as a question.

"Everything. When you tell me to take care of something, I do it."

All the kids have an admirable work ethic. We made them each go out and get after-school or weekend jobs when they were twelve. Now, that discipline is embedded. When they finish a task, they all have an "Okay, what *else* can I do?" attitude. Not one of them is spoiled. The success that each of them is enjoying in the work world does not surprise me.

Ella Reilly, Brian's daughter with his wife Lisa, is the apple of her parents' eyes, and Mary Ann's and mine.

I could retire, Mary Ann and I could. But what would I do all day? It's not about the money. I spent a lot of my life not having money.

And there's so much still to do. Recently, through my involvement with the National Leadership Academy, I sponsored six underprivileged students from Philadelphia to fly to an enrichment program in Colorado that featured speakers on leadership, on how to go through life with a positive attitude, that sort of thing. The response from the students was unbelievable, and achieved what you would hope: an experience different enough to instill in them a new perspective, enough to change and better their lives.

That's six young people. There are more out there.

I'm blessed to know truly how short and fragile life is. One day you're playing street hockey with your buddies, the next they're slicing skin from your leg and laying it on your face, hoping it will take.

People still stare. That never changes. In truth, I may notice it more now as I've gone through the process of writing this book and really looking at what my life has added up to. On a recent business trip to New York, I walked from my hotel to a nearby SoulCycle. It was very early in the morning, so not many people were out on the street, but each one who was, looked. Maybe crowds are actually better because I can't register *everyone* who stares. At SoulCycle, there were ten people in the class; everyone looked. Maybe things were always like this and I just succeeded in blocking it out when I was younger so I could accomplish what I needed. Now, I see what my kids were going through when they were younger: they may have had the more accurate sense of what was going on while I was busy steeling myself and them against it. Like I said, I wouldn't be where I am without thick skin. Anyway, even if my eyes are more open now, I can't completely change my approach to the staring. Most of the time I'll let it slide, though if it persists beyond some reasonable point, I'll glare back and say something like, "Really, dude? What's up?"

The one thing I think I never quite did in all these years until now: mourn the life of young Brian Walsh, the life he never had because of that fire. I never gave him a proper burial in my mind. Without that, it's hard to let go of the loss and move on. I think of that scene in *The Shawshank Redemption*, when 'Red' Redding, the longtime prison inmate played so beautifully by Morgan Freeman, sits before the parole board once again, after years and years of having his parole denied, and talks with such honesty and resignation about how he wishes, as an old man who knows what he now knows, that he could speak to that young man he once was. "But I can't," he says. "That kid's long gone."

Alright then. Let all these be the words by the graveside that were never actually said because he did not technically die. Because he grew up to be me, someone he might never have been.

AFTERWORD

New Orleans, June 2005.

My name is called.

I walk out to center stage of the enormous Convention Center hall. The applause is pretty enthusiastic, I must admit, like thunder. Wow. So this is what it sounds like to have nine thousand people clapping and rooting for you.

I've been asked to speak by the Million Dollar Round Table, the largest organization in the world for financial professionals.

Yes, I've been professionally successful. But let's be honest. I'm also up here because of what I look like.

I survey the sea of faces. There, down in front, are the most important ones: Mary Ann, Brian, Matt, and Katie. The kids are ages seventeen, fifteen, and thirteen. I recognize many other faces—colleagues, friends, the terrific event organizers. The teleprompter is cued up. So are the graphics that will be projected on the screen behind me to show everyone what I looked like, before and right after. I hope no one passes out. For the second time ever, I'll be talking publicly about my personal life, what it's been like for me. This time I can add some of the important lessons I've learned.

Everyone should have such an opportunity. The one time your life gets summed up shouldn't be at your funeral, when you're not there to hear it.

The applause subsides. They're all looking up at me, waiting. From what I see, the world does not appear different than it did that night so many years ago. It's lots of faces, all kinds of faces, regular faces.

No, the big change, the profound, amazing change, is what the world sees. They look at me differently.

And I like it.

ACKNOWLEDGMENTS

Wow.

Writing this book has been quite the journey. It brought back all kinds of emotions from my original harrowing journey—great sadness and great happiness, too. The opportunity to tell my story could not have been accomplished without the help of many people. I would like to thank:

Mitch Ostrove, who originally encouraged me that my story needed to be told.

My nephew Ed Walsh, who has been by my side through this whole process, providing great input and feedback.

Tommy Spaulding, who convinced me that the world needs more authentic stories so that people can hope.

Michael Palgon, who made me dig deep to find "the Story." Michael also guided me to one of the most incredible human beings I have ever dealt with, Andrew Postman.

Andrew Postman, who brought this story to life in ways I could never have done alone. I learned a lot from Andrew: how to be open and vulnerable to tell that authentic story; to speak from my heart, which, among other things, enabled me to share the lessons I have learned; and, most importantly, to see that we can always make new friends who bring meaning to our lives.

My late Dad and my Mom, relentless supporters of my recovery. Their love got me through those tough early months. It was not until I became a parent myself that I truly understood what they went through.

My siblings, who were constant visitors to the burn center. I always knew they were there, and each of them being there meant everything to me. Patty, my "sister cousin," was an inspiring role model, helping me to get through those days and also to imagine better days ahead. She encouraged each path I chose, even those she may have thought were not necessarily the best.

The late Jim and Millie Clark, who treated me as their son. They were each an inspiration and a role model for me.

Everyone in my office who helped to create Walsh & Nicholson Financial Group. The work we do for our clients is indeed extraordinary. Kevin Nicholson, my partner of twenty-eight years, has shared with me, and I'm sure will continue to share with me, an incredible ride full of laughs, angst, and love of family. Amy Wintz-Murphy has been, without question, the best assistant I could ever have asked for, and I am truly blessed to have her in my life.

The late John T. Glasson, and Ken Sims: without these two heroic men saving my life, nothing would have been possible.

My wife Mary Ann, who initially did everything she could to avoid me until she finally gave in when my charm and wit got the best of her. Mary Ann is a beautiful person, a wonderful mother, and the most loving, supportive, best friend I could ever have dreamed of.

Our children, Brian, Matthew, and Kathryn, who fill us with so much pride at the way they have all turned out, and who make us proud every single day. We love Lisa like a daughter, and for being such a terrific mother.

Our granddaughters, Ella Reilly Walsh and Joie James Walsh, who represent our revenge on Brian and Lisa!

High school graduation photo, two weeks
before the accident. October 1981.

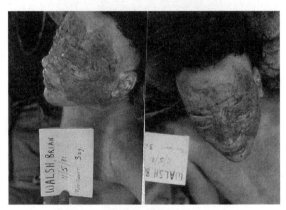

Three days post-first graft and after being
extubated. November 5, 1981.

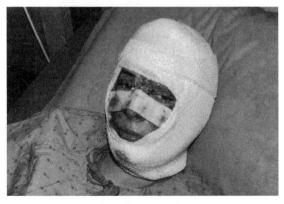

Post-second graft. November 16, 1981.

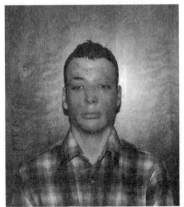

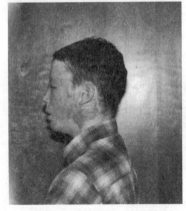

Before mask. January 1982.

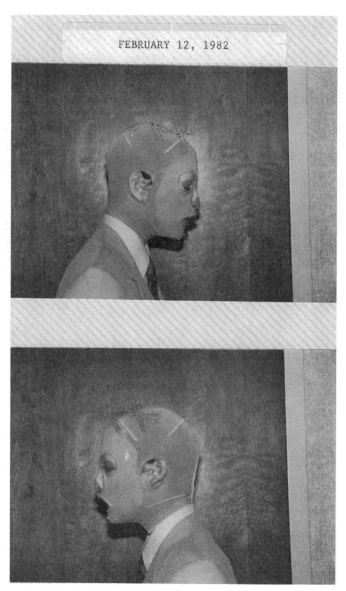

One month into wearing mask
and insert. February 1982.

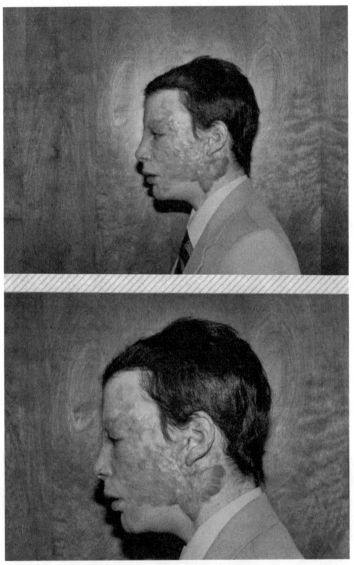

One month after wearing mask.
February 1982.

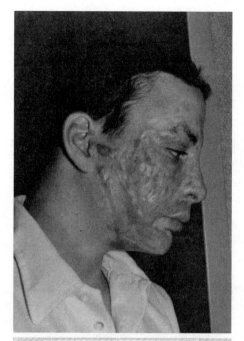

AUGUST 10, 1982

Seven months after wearing mask.
Summer 1982.

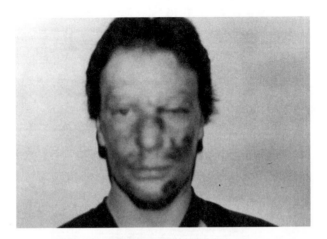

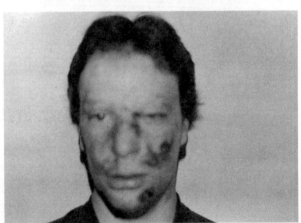

Eyelid clipped shut for six months after eyelid graft.
Lip graft, several z-plasties, and dermabrasions.

Family vacation to Palm Springs. Top: Lisa, Matthew.
Bottom: Me, Mary Ann, Katie, Brian Jr. December 2015.

Annual cutting down of Christmas tree.
Left to right: Katie, Matthew, Lisa, Brian Jr.

My Ameritas Hall of Fame induction, Banff, Canada.
Left to right: Matthew, Katie, Brian Jr.

Katie's college graduation. Left to right: Mary Ann,
Brian Jr., Lisa, Katie, Matthew, and me. May 2014.

Ella and me. September 2019.

Ella and Joie, my two granddaughters.
January 2020.

Me, Ella, Brian Jr., and Matthew.
January 2020.

Me with Joie and Ella.
February 2020.